Memories of
Ancient Israel

Also by Philip R. Davies

Scribes and Schools: The Canonization of the Hebrew Scriptures
(Library of Ancient Israel)

Memories of Ancient Israel

An Introduction to Biblical History—Ancient and Modern

Philip R. Davies

Westminster John Knox Press
LOUISVILLE • LONDON

Scripture quotations from the New Revised Standard Version of the Bible are copyright © 1989 by the Division of Christian Education of the National Council of the Churches of Christ in the U.S.A. and are used by permission.

Book design by Sharon Adams
Cover design by Jennifer K. Cox

First edition
Published by Westminster John Knox Press
Louisville, Kentucky

This book is printed on acid-free paper that meets the American National Standards Institute Z39.48 standard. ∞

PRINTED IN THE UNITED STATES OF AMERICA

08 09 10 11 12 13 14 15 16 17—10 9 8 7 6 5 4 3 2 1

Library of Congress Cataloging-in-Publication Data

Davies, Philip R.
    Memories of ancient Israel : an introduction to biblical history—ancient and modern / Philip R. Davies.
        p. cm.
    Includes index.
    ISBN 978-0-664-23288-7 (alk. paper)
    1. Bible. O.T.—History of Biblical events.   2. Bible. O.T.—Antiquities.
3. Palestine—History—To 70 A.D.—Historiography.   4. Bible. O.T.—Criticism, interpretation, etc.   I. Title.
    BS1197.D38 2008
    221.9'5—dc22

                                                                2008013187

Contents

Acknowledgments   ix

1. *Bible, History, and "Biblical History"*   1
   "Biblical History"   1
   The Biblical Historian   5
   Bible   6
   History   9
   "The Bible as History"   15
   Summary   17

PART ONE: RESOURCES

2. *Bible I: Chronology, Facts, and Causality*   21
   Chronology   21
      The Monarchs of Israel and Judah   21
      Before the Monarchs, and After   27
   Facts   32
   Causality   42
   Summary   45

3. *Bible II: "Israel"*   47
   First and Second Histories   47
   Fluctuating Biblical Israels   50

Which "Israel" Belongs in a Modern History?   55
Summary   56

4. *Archaeology: Use and Abuse*   58
    The Rise and Fall of Biblical Archaeology   60
    Postbiblical Archaeology?   66
    Archaeological Practice   68
        Urban Excavation   69
        Example: The Problem of the United Monarchy   74
    Survey, Demography, Ecology   76
        Judah and Jerusalem in
            the Eighth–Seventh Centuries   78
        The Neo-Babylonian and Persian Period:
            Jerusalem to Mizpah and Back   79
    Ethnicity   81
    Summary   82

5. *Epigraphic Sources*   85
    Inscriptions and Chronology   86
    Documentary Texts   87
    Monumental Inscriptions   88
    Inscriptions Relating to Biblical History   90
        The Merneptah Stele   90
        Shalmaneser III and Sennacherib   91
        Judah and the Neo-Babylonians   93
        The Mesha Inscription   94
        The Tel Dan Stele   95
        The Siloam Inscription   97
    Forgeries   98
    Summary   99
    Conclusion to Part One   100

PART TWO: STRATEGIES

6. *Cultural Memory*   105
    On Remembering History   106
    The Bible as Judean Cultural Memory   111

Cultural Memory in Practice: Ezra and Nehemiah   115
Summary   122

7. *Knowledge, Judgment, Belief*   124
Verification   126
Correlating Literature and Archaeology   128
Reliability   130
Probability   136
Belief   141
"What Did the Biblical Writers Know?"   141
Summary   142

8. *A Tale of Two Histories*   145
The Minimalist Option   147
The Maximalist Option   149
Biblical History in Recent Debate   150
The Maximalist Thesis   156
Jens Bruun Kofoed   157
Iain Provan, V. Phillips Long,
and Tremper Longman   158
Kenneth Kitchen   164
Summary   169

PART THREE: REFLECTIONS

9. *History, Memory, and Theology*   175

Index of Ancient Sources   179

Index of Names   181

Acknowledgments

Apart from me, the person who has suffered most during the production of this book is my wife, Birgit Maenz-Davies, who patiently lets me talk all day to the computer and keeps me sane the rest of the time.

I also have to thank my colleague Diana Edelman for continued stimulation on the topic of history and for numerous suggestions (and corrections), mostly during a very busy teaching schedule. I am grateful, too, to Jim West for his comments and corrections.

Chapter One

Bible, History, and "Biblical History"

Historical study is not the study of the past but the study of
present traces of the past. (Elton 2002, 8)

"Biblical History"

I hope that people with quite different backgrounds and interests
will come across this book. But I assume the reader will be interested in either the Bible or history, or both. In this first chapter,
then, let us look at "Bible" and "history" together and separately.

"Biblical history" is generally used to mean the times and places
to which the biblical stories about the past refer. In the same way,
we speak of "biblical lands" or "biblical archaeology" or even "the
biblical period." Such usage does not necessarily imply any difference of quality attaching to these times and places: they still
form part of a wider human history. But the fact that they come
within the Bible's purview does afford them a special place in the
modern, Western world. Our civilization has been nurtured in
many ways by stories of that time and place: we 'remember' it in
our culture. For Jews this story tells us of the people whom the
one Creator God chose for himself, while for many Christians it
tells of a divine preparation for the coming of the world's Savior.
Such beliefs tend to imbue the biblical story with a certain aura.
It has often been referred to as "sacred history."

Christian theology was at the center of medieval European scholarship, and biblical history was part of its curriculum. That is still largely the case within Western culture. The study of biblical history is still found almost entirely within faculties of divinity and theology. Meanwhile, however, the academic study of history has also entered into schools and universities, and brought with it ways of understanding and interpreting the past that can broadly be called humanistic or secular. While biblical history remains institutionally rather isolated from the study of history generally, its modern practitioners have more and more adapted their scholarship to this secular view, in which history is the story of the human past and the human past interacts globally: all histories, including those to which the Bible refers, interlock. Biblical history operates at the present time as a subdiscipline of historical studies and of Christian theology (or Jewish studies). In some institutions it resembles the kind of history taught elsewhere; in others it is still treated as of special significance to Jews or Christians.

This dual character extends beyond the academic world into the public arena, where Bible history also enjoys a special place, both as a record of an ancient world for which there is a widespread fascination—the ancient civilizations of Babylon, Egypt, Greece, and Rome all belong with or closely beside biblical history—and also as part of an inherited religious or cultural world. The large media output devoted to showing how the biblical stories really are history is undoubtedly fueled by strong religious belief, but it also feeds a cultural commitment to a "real" past.

The modern secular discipline of history is in tension with notions of sacred history, in which the divine hand is perceived. But the Bible itself, and the theologies that it has engendered, in its turn challenges the humanistic discipline of history. The Bible claims—for the most part—that God is the controller not just of sacred history but of all history, always and everywhere. The movements of the great empires of Egypt and Assyria and Persia, it tells us, are orchestrated by Israel's God. What are referred to as "the nations" are also part of God's divine plan.

Historians of ancient Egypt or Iraq, working in a Middle Eastern or history department, are unaffected by such claims, unless they are employed within a religious institution. The notion that the God of Israel (or any other god, for that matter) plays a role in the politics of the ancient Middle East is simply not considered. The modern, secular understanding of history is based on the principle that historical events are shaped by natural forces and human actions, both individual and collective. That is how historical explanation works. If the past—or even a part of it—can be explained by the workings of a god, then there is in principle no history arising from purely human action: humans become not subjects of the historical process but objects. There is an additional practical difficulty with divine intervention or control: once this factor is allowed into historical explanation, it is uncontrollable. Victorious generals and nations used to claim that the gods were on their side and helped them to conquer. But no modern historian, to my knowledge, suggested that the Allies won the 1939–45 war because of divine help, even if both sides prayed to God for succor. Yet the Bible's view of history persists among those modern religious believers who regard their God as having a plan for their personal life; some also believe that their God has a plan for the world. Now, if human activity does not determine the outcome of events, but rather a divine will, then history is just a ticking clock, marking an invisible time and nothing else. Studying history is futile: it is a charade. But in places where biblical history is taught, this notion of a divine purpose in history remains and challenges the secular understanding of history.

The modern historian does not have to rule out the possibility of divine intervention in the course of human or natural affairs: if there is a God, or gods, he or she or they may very well intervene. But if such a belief is embedded in the historian's work, then biblical history is detached from all other pasts with which modern historians deal. A solution may lie in keeping separate a secular history of ancient Palestine (or even of Israel and Judah) taught as part of world history, and biblical history taught as part of theology. There is a context for this kind of disciplinary division in universities that include both a school of divinity and a school of religion. Ancient Israel and Judah would then be studied on the one hand as kingdoms and populations within Palestine of the first millennium BCE and on the other hand as the people whose story forms part of the religious belief and theological curriculum of Judaism and Christianity or a Christian story revealing in some way the divine character and purpose. A quite different situation exists within the modern state of Israel, where the biblical story is taught in schools as a secular national history. That system is generating serious conflict with the study of history and archaeology in some Jewish universities.

Is it satisfactory either to separate a religious and a secular version of ancient Israelite and Judean history? Most modern theologians do not in fact wish to quarrel with secular historians over the principles of historical research, even if their theology might lead them to a different understanding of what historical explanation ultimately might be. A few biblical historians argue strenuously for the substantial or even complete historicity of the biblical accounts, but whatever their private motivation, they now argue explicitly on empirical or philosophical grounds. Sometimes, however, the dogmatic foundation is visible, as in debate about the book of Daniel. According to most scholars, following a very ancient critique by the non-Christian philosopher Porphyry, the writer of the book was not the sixth-century exile himself, but its authors (or at least its final editors) lived in the second century BCE, as shown by historical errors. To some this circumstance made the book a fraud. This accusation is revealing; from a secular perspective the Bible is not under judgment, and in the ancient (including the Jewish) world, pseudepigraphy was so common that it was surely recognized and accepted as such. The charge implies a belief in biblical "honesty." But critical historians determine historicity by rational means and neither attack nor defend the ancient literature for not being infallible. Nevertheless, the persistence of the language of defending and attacking or believing and doubting the Bible certainly betrays something more religious than academic taking place below the surface, sometimes even when it is accepted that biblical history should be studied like other history. I briefly consider theology in relation to history in this book's final chapter, but it does not belong to my account of how history should be done, including biblical history.

The Biblical Historian

The difficulties of biblical history are practical as well as method-ological. A standard history of ancient Israel and Judah—or even of ancient Palestine—cannot disregard the Bible. This collection of ancient texts is a major resource, and indeed a double resource. First, it gives stories about the past. Those stories may be false, true, or a mixture of fact and fiction, but the historian has to eval-uate them. Second, the texts telling the stories are the most impor-tant and influential products of the ancient history of Palestine, and the historian has to explain how they came to be created and preserved. This second aspect is in fact a particularly secular con-cern: theological study is less inclined to regard the Bible purely exclusively as an outcome of ancient human history, but an evalu-ation of the biblical texts as historical sources cannot possibly be undertaken without considering them as historical products.

Whether the history of ancient Palestine should be left to bibli-cal scholars is another matter. Keith Whitelam (1996) has argued strongly that it should not, and with good reason. Palestine is much more than ancient Israel and, especially nowadays, has to serve more than one constituency. But the historian of Judah and Israel in the first millennium BCE has to become a biblical scholar as well, and, to be a "normal" historian, must be a secular biblical scholar. But if such scholars exist now (and they do), they come not from the ranks of modern historians, but of biblical scholars. But biblical studies has emerged over the last century or so as a subject that can be pursued independently of theology, and indeed a self-consciously secular agenda for this discipline has become increasingly evident. In some cases, this agenda is strongly antireligious, but such antagonism is not necessary; many scholars accept, implicitly or explicitly, that study of the Bible has to be to some degree secularized.

A tracking of twentieth-century histories of ancient Israel will show how the genre has become more and more secular, prompted especially by the introduction of archaeological data. We shall see later (chap. 4) that while archaeology was at first used simply to illustrate the biblical story, it has gradually come to modify and even contest that story. If the discipline of history has not tried to lift historical study of the Bible from its traditional disciplinary niche, then many biblical historians have broken out in the direction of secular history.

Given that modern biblical history, for reasons of scholarly competence, requires a practitioner who is a biblical scholar as well as a historian, such practitioners generally work within the context of biblical studies. This book is written about this practice, and for such practitioners.

Let me, then, sum up what I mean by biblical history and the biblical historian. Both terms relate to a discipline that accepts the secular principles of modern historical study which understand that a historian can only deal with the past as an arena of human action and causality (with a certain degree of natural, but not divine, input). Biblical history is not the same as the history of ancient Palestine, in which the Bible is interested only patchily. Biblical history is the study of the Bible as a source of historical knowledge about ancient Israel and Judah and as a product of historical processes within ancient Israel and Judah. As such, it requires of the practitioner a competence in the scholarly study of the Bible. Biblical history is a subdiscipline of history and biblical studies, and needs to exploit the methods and competencies of both.

Before leaving this part of the introduction, I should note the recent and important book by Megan Bishop Moore (2006), which is, like this one, devoted to the question of whether and how biblical history should be written. The general approach that Moore takes is quite similar to mine, though often using different categories, and the reader may well find it helpful to compare her presentation with the one given here. The book came into my possession too late to be considered, but, like this one, it comes to the conclusion that there are broadly two methodological options. I deal with these options in chapter 8, where I comment briefly on Moore's treatment of them.

Bible

I assume in this book that the reader is familiar with the Bible, but in this section I want to make it clear that the historian must recognize bibles themselves, and not just their stories, as products of human historical action. The word "bible" comes from Greek, then Latin *biblia*, both being plural nouns meaning "books" (or "scrolls"). The singular meaning has arisen only since these books were bound together into a single volume, known as a codex, the form of the modern book. The earliest Bible codices to have survived (and quite probably among the earliest manufactured) date from the fourth century CE, are Christian, and were written in Greek. There were no Jewish Bibles in this sense until the Middle Ages.

What of their contents? While a fixed Jewish list of books that in the language of the rabbis "defiled the hands" (i.e., they were "sacred") had very probably emerged by the first century CE, the contents of Christian Bibles have never been fixed. The simple way to illustrate this is to compare the lists of contents of the three earliest Bible codices—Sinaiticus, Vaticanus, and Alexandrinus—then the original King James Version and any Roman Catholic Bible. These all include books (the Apocrypha or deuterocanonical books) absent from the Jewish Scriptures. Later editions of the KJV omit these books, reflecting a disagreement about whether they are really canonical. Finally compare the New Revised Standard Version, which has the apocryphal books, including Additions to Esther, as a separate item. Outside the West, the Scriptures of the Ethiopian Orthodox Church constitute both a broader and a narrower canon, the broader canon including the books of Jubilees and Enoch—and many other smaller differences from Western canons. The Bibles of other Orthodox churches also vary from the Bibles of the West. Biblical history is more extensive, and indeed more internally contradictory, in these Orthodox Bibles. The order of books and the text of the books also varies. Bibles are books containing the scriptural canons of various Christian communities, the result of human decisions made by different people in different times and places. There is no single Bible and strictly speaking no absolutely fixed biblical history. It also follows that there are no biblical authors, only authors (and editors) of works that were later canonized as Scripture (though in this book I shall use the term as a convenient shorthand).

The structure of biblical canons also differs. The Jewish Bible—according to an ancient convention dating to probably no later than the first century CE—consists of three divisions: Torah (Law), Prophets, and Writings. The books of Kings are within the divisions of Prophets, but Chronicles is in Writings; Ezra and Nehemiah are also in Writings, but they precede Chronicles. The stories of the patriarchs, exodus, and lawgiving are part of Torah. Historical books are not indicated either by classification or ordering. It is the Christian Old Testament, the Septuagint, that arranges the Old Testament books by genre, separating the former Prophets (Joshua–Kings), inserting into them Ruth, following them by Chronicles and Esther and the books of Maccabees, thus making a sequence of historical books which, according to some patristic authorities, included the Pentateuch.

One further consideration needs to be introduced, since it is important for the next chapter. Several different textual versions of the Hebrew Bible/Old Testament have survived. Among the Dead Sea Scrolls, from the third century BCE to the first century CE, there are even more versions. The (Masoretic) Jewish text has been standardized for about two thousand years and forms the basis of the Christian Vulgate version and of modern translations, both Jewish and Christian. The original Christian biblical text and the text used by the majority of Jews in the ancient world, who did not read Hebrew, is based on Hebrew texts that sometimes differ from the Masoretic text. The Samaritan text, which includes only the Pentateuch (yes, a different Bible for Samaritans, too), is also in Hebrew but does not correspond to the Masoretic version exactly. While the differences between the three texts are usually minor, they often diverge in the matter of chronology, obliging the historian to bear in mind that the biblical writings themselves have not only a literary history but a textual one too.

What, then, does "Bible" mean in *this* book? I have chosen the books of the Jewish Scriptures, which also form in their content, though not their sequence, the Protestant Old Testament. Since "Old Testament" and "Hebrew Bible" are not ideal terms, I have decided to use "Bible," and I shall not be dealing with the very interesting problems of doing history from the New Testament.

Had I chosen to use the NRSV as my Bible, I would have included Tobit, Judith, and 1–2 Maccabees. The two books of Maccabees must date to the second or first centuries BCE, and 2 Maccabees is agreed to have been written in Greek. I have never come across a defense of the historicity of any of these, though 1 Maccabees is usually regarded as being fairly reliable, if clearly propagandistic. But Judith would have required some very extensive discussion, for among other historical impossibilities, it opens with the words, "It was the twelfth year of the reign of Nebuchadnezzar, who ruled over the Assyrians in the great city of Nineveh."

History

Now I want to show that just as a Bible is a human product, so is history. But we have to be aware that "history" is used to mean three things: the past, a story about the past, and the study of the past (or, as Elton would have it, the past in the present). Quite often in modern discussion of history it is not clear which sense is meant, and sometimes the three are confused. Some explanation is needed of how these three usages relate.

Let us start with history as the past. For me, the term "history" implies some form or meaning, though it may not for others, and as such suggests something more than simply "the past." But at any rate, "the past," seen as whatever has been before the present, has no intrinsic shape or meaning. Raw data do not interpret themselves. Even turning them into facts may involve interpretation. In any case, we have knowledge of only a small part of the past. How could we deduce anything but a partial meaning from the little that we know?

History is more correctly understood in the second sense, as a story about the past—about the past with *meaning*. We humans provide the meaning that we discern in the past, which turns events into history in this second sense. A clap of thunder that no one hears makes no noise; a rose has no color. We see and hear everything by turning air waves and light waves into images and sounds. We thus create both color and sound, and we know that some animals turn certain frequencies into sounds and colors that we do not. We can certainly talk about objects making sounds and having colors, but we also know that strictly speaking they do not produce these. They merely produce waves. Sound and color are the results of how our organs process external stimuli. In exactly the same way, humans also understand events through the organ of narrative (or story). We select and organize data into sequences and clusters. We connect the acts of a person and construct from them a personality; we choose certain events, focus on them in a certain way, and so manufacture a plot. The illusion we create is that such a story is there, objectively, that it *is* the past, just as we believe that sounds are really there. But without ears there is no sound and without story there is no history. The question of what happened always invites a narrative.

But nowadays we do not call just any story about the past "history." It must relate something that really happened. Yet the data we have about the past can vary tremendously in quality and quantity, and so, correspondingly, does our knowledge of "what actually happened." A modern historian writing about recent history may have a huge amount of data, which will restrict the kind of history that can be told but also enable that history to accommodate a wide range of facts; there is less capacity for "fiction." Ancient historians, however, were usually faced with nothing but stories already told by others; they rarely had access to archives, archaeology, or eyewitnesses. If we have no direct data from the past, we can—and indeed we must—rely on these stories and on our own imagination and reasoning. We cannot vouch for anything that we write. However much an ancient historian might try to discover what had happened earlier, the outcome could not be history in our modern, restricted definition. It will contain what we would now designate as myth, legend, gossip, and rumor, all created through the recycling and embellishment of others' stories.

The modern biblical historian is in many respects in a similar predicament. We have no shortage of stories in the Bible, but we cannot guarantee to ourselves or our readers how much fact these stories contain—or indeed how much the writers of these stories themselves could vouch for what they wrote. We do know that sometimes records were kept of ancestors, kings, and officials (see next chapter), which might enable a story to rely upon some data. But what we now understand by "history" and "historian" cannot be usefully applied—or argued about—for people who had no direct data about the past, as opposed to stories about the past, of which no doubt there were also plenty. No doubt these stories contained information that would have corresponded to what we would recognize as facts if we could only know. But until we can turn the data into facts, we cannot tell a story that corresponds to them.

A great deal of rather silly argument can be carried on over whether the writers of stories in the Bible are historians. On the one hand, it is perhaps a little unfair not to allow that they were possibly trying to represent what they thought was a real past. On the other hand, if by calling them "historians" we give the impression that they knew about the past and could describe it accurately, we should avoid the term. The fact is that their intentions to write history and their competence to do so are quite separate matters. We can judge them as historians on either criterion, but the one does not entail the other!

The historian is not, of course, merely a teller of facts. Stories are never innocent of point of view, plot, ideology, or cultural value. We tell our stories of the past in a historical context, looking at the past from a particular point: the present. We cannot be objective, neutral observers. We ourselves are in history, in the sense both of events happening and of the stories (news, gossip, history books) that interpret these events—not to mention our own memories. That historical viewpoint shifts all the time, and as it shifts our view of the past lengthens and adjusts. Modern histories of slavery or warfare are quite different from those of two centuries ago, and the attention we now pay to the role of women, for example, is more than it used to be.

Our views of the past are also affected by our geographical, political, and social location. Until recently a good deal of history writing was national and chauvinistic: in my own early reading the British were usually the heroes and foreigners the villains. It has now become more common for Western nations at least to recognize their own past faults—genocides, massacres, enslavements, treacheries, and sheer ineptitude—although there are still some countries where such episodes are forgotten or even denied. In Ireland there are memories of the great potato famine that drove thousands abroad. This episode was never taught to me in school as part of English colonial misrule. I could name English Protestant martyrs and knew about the Inquisition, but I could not name a Catholic martyr except Guy Fawkes, and he was not represented as a martyr but a villain who tried to kill a Protestant king. In Northern Ireland, Protestants still notoriously celebrate great Protestant victories and wear orange after the Protestant king William (of Orange). Catholics are more likely to celebrate the 1916 Easter uprising against British rule. Closer to our own topic, the zealots who suffered the Roman siege of Masada at the end of the Jewish rebellion are celebrated in Israel as freedom fighters. To the Romans (and their adopted Jewish historian Josephus) they were brigands, bandits, terrorists.

In America, too, various histories compete: those who live in Canada remember rather different events than do those in the United States, while the film genre of the western has exported across the world a certain memory of "how the West was won" and celebrated the virtues that supposedly won it. These images reflect and shape the cultural values of Americans, including its tolerance of gun ownership, which horrifies most Europeans. Those descended from the aboriginal Americans (who used to be called "red Indians") are more likely to remember how the West was lost. None of these differences or memories need to involve disputes over the actual data, or even of the implied fact. They generate often bitter dissent over what they mean, and they mean different things to different people.

The simple lesson to learn is that our stories about the past may well shed light on the past itself, but they shed a colored light as well as shedding light on us. A lot of what I have just been describing may have been once regarded as history, but we might now refer to it rather as cultural memory—stories about the past shared by people who affirm a common identity, and who use stories to reinforce that identity. The Bible's narratives are a supreme example of this: they convey above all a story of a national identity. But translating this identity can cause problems. Modern Jews, and especially Israelis, obviously find it natural. Many Christians also appropriate Israel to their own identity through their understanding of the New Testament. But I once had several conversations with a Christian monk in Jerusalem who had been entrusted with the task of preparing a liturgy for Christian Palestinian Arabs of the Anglican denomination. Palestinian Christians, whose view of Israel is as an intruding and occupying regime, can no longer identify even liturgically with the people of God or worship the god of Israel. There is a clash of modern identities in modern Palestine in which Christians elsewhere can become implicated. Biblical history lives on as cultural memories, and the modern biblical historian has to recognize and deal with that issue. The traces of the past are not only material but persist in the form of stories that may or may not be true but which carry identities with them. Identity is one of the key chains from which we construct stories of the past.

The final meaning of "history" is the most modern: the critical study of the past. I have suggested that before the arrival of history as a scholarly discipline it was cultural memory, group memory, memories that create identity and solidarity that conveyed our knowledge and belief about the past (and that still happens). The critical historian can, and should, generate stories of the past that we can count as historical knowledge. But critical history can also scrutinize cultural memories, confronting them where they are factually wrong and exposing their biases. Historians can never compose a "correct" history; there can be no such thing. But they must make clear that not all stories about the past count as history in the sense of knowledge.

In what sense can we gain historical knowledge? By what rules does a historian judge, or create, a critical account of the past? First, and most straightforwardly, by being attentive to all the data, the traces of the past in the present. These, as I have said, do not of themselves deliver a history, but they can be arranged into coherence by means of argument, inference, and deduction. Coherence and probability also play a role. Does the account make sense of how we think human affairs work? These rules exert some control over what we accept as historical knowledge, but no more. Every account, however critical, emphasizes certain data, derives facts, entertains certain possibilities, and assesses the roles and influence of principal characters. These judgments are subjective, though not arbitrary if derived from evidence and argument.

Historical knowledge cannot, however, be scientific. Even the most conscientious historians have to be wrong in their reconstruction of the past. In deciding that a particular event occurred or was the outcome of a particular cause, the historian presents what seems—by whatever calculation—to be most probable. Yet we all know that improbable things occur. So a history that relies on the probable always happening cannot always be right. Nevertheless, no critical historian can say, "I know that I am suggesting something improbable, but improbable things sometimes happen and this is one of them." If the historian can argue that despite its improbability, it did occur, then in effect the argument is that *in this case the event was probable*. We can contrast this with fiction, in which the reader is perfectly happy to accept improbability and coincidence. What happens in a novel is what the author says happens. We do not believe this of a historian, who is supposedly telling us what happened. But—this is important—historical knowing is not scientific. We can know data, even facts; we can certainly conclude what we don't know, and eliminate inaccurate accounts of the past. The rest—reconstruction—is a different kind of knowledge, one that belongs typically to the social sciences.

Like all modern academic disciplines, the practice of critical history has engendered a good deal of theoretical debate. There are excellent discussions of the issues by Elton (2002), Appleby, Hunt, and Jacob (1994), and Fulbrook (2002). Much of the debate focuses on how history is scientific. My own opinion is that history can usefully be compared with architecture. Both rely on scientific principles, or else their structures will collapse. But just as architecture is functional sculpture, and except at its very worst strives for some kind of aesthetic effect, a history is also literature. There is no single solution to an architectural challenge. We judge the result by whether it works. All history takes the form of a story, and storytelling is an art. We are at least partly persuaded by the aesthetic or philosophical qualities of a history as well as by its power in making sense of facts. The best-known analysis of history as narrative is Hayden White's *Metahistory* (1973), in which he shows four different plots that a history can have: romance, satire, comedy, and tragedy. Whether he is ultimately correct in his analysis, he shows very clearly how history functions as rhetoric.

"The Bible as History"

I hope it is clear from the preceding discussion that neither "Bible" nor "history" are fixed, objective phenomena, but are constructed by humans within the course of human events, and vary from time to time, place to place, and community to community. The biblical historian must also realize that in ancient Israel or Judah there was neither Bible nor critical history; we are imposing later categories.

Hans Frei, in his *The Eclipse of Biblical Narrative*, demonstrates how in the Middle Ages the Bible provided the great mythic narrative in which the personal and social life of the Christian believer was enveloped, starting with the fall from grace and innocence by the wickedness of Satan, through to the final judgment of the soul (or resurrected body) and the defeat of Satan. Within this narrative, individual Bible stories and persons could also be read as figures of aspects of everyday life, applying moral lessons. This biblical world functioned as the template of reality, and everyday life was measured by it. But in the eighteenth century this approach was reversed: instead of everyday life being enveloped in the biblical world, the everyday world became the real world and enveloped the Bible: it provided the means of measuring it. So the Bible became rationalized: it was held either to speak universal truths or to relate historical events. Instead of the biblical narrative world being greater than human experience, it became smaller: its realism became historical reality. We might say the biblical narrative lost its mythic quality and thus its direct hold on the worldview of the Christian believer.

The evolution of the modern critical notion of history as a story of real past events is nicely charted by Diane Banks (2006), who also discusses the impact of these developments on modern biblical history. In particular, she underlines the philosophical differences between Germany and the United States during the twentieth century. In Germany, the historicist view upheld the uniqueness of every historical event and the need to understand and explain its unique historical context. In the United States, the influence of the social sciences on historical research and writing led to a search for general principles that could be applied to individual cases. The historicist position was conducive to detailed examination of sources in search of the unique character of past events, while the social-scientific position was more conducive to ideas of patterning and evolution. The great European sociologists Weber and Marx were paradoxically more influential across the Atlantic than on their own continent.

Slogans like "the Bible as History" (as in the 1956 book by Werner Keller) are typical of an approach that couples an uncritical concept of Bible with a critical understanding of history as a story about a real past. For example, certain distinctions cannot really be avoided. If the Bible is history, what about the creation, the flood, and Jonah's big fish? Are there stories about the past in the Bible that are not about the real past, not history? How do you tell the difference? We can sometimes demonstrate the historicity of the Bible by appealing to external sources, but these do not help us at all with the stories of Ruth, Jonah, or Esther. If we want to make a distinction between story and history (as our postmedieval world does), we can do so only by some literary evaluation, in the way that we recognize the parables of Jesus as stories and not as real events. This judgment implies a critical examination of the Bible. Now, even before the nineteenth century, when Leopold von Ranke completed the foundations of modern critical history, devout Christian Bible readers had begun to notice variations in the narratives of Genesis that led them to suggest the author, Moses, had used sources. The pursuit of source criticism led, as is well known, to a reconstruction of the history of Israelite religion quite different from that offered in the Bible: the elaborate Mosaic legislation came not at the beginning, but the end. Once the biblical texts come to be read literally, they also come to be read critically. But, as I have said, this is an intrinsic part of the biblical historian's task of understanding the production of the biblical stories.

For that reason, the modern historian does not discard stories that are judged not to relate real events. All stories are products of history. We may interpret many biblical stories about the past as being instructive and not literally descriptive. Jonah can be understood as a fable about universalism, or bigotry, or even about divine whimsy, and Ruth as a tract about intermarriage or a legend about the origins of David's ancestry. Esther has a less obvious moral meaning, but can be understood as an explanation of the feast of Purim. Stories of a six-day creation, a primeval paradise, and a universal flood can be understood as myth. It is important to recognize that biblical texts have more than one way of writing about the past—ways that we would not call "history." Indeed, history in our modern sense cannot be one of those ways. But the modern historian should be interested in any way of writing about the past, and especially in the significance of stories about the past for those who told and heard those stories.

Summary

I have not tried in this opening chapter to give more than a sketchy account of the main issues (as I see them) confronting the modern biblical historian. What I have tried to show are some of the presuppositions about Bible and history that need to be recognized before dealing with the Bible as history. In particular, I have stressed that there are two distinct but closely related tasks. One is to clarify what the relationship is between the various biblical narratives about the past and what we can know (in the historical sense) of the real past. The other is to clarify those narratives as products of that real past. It is a more complicated enterprise than appears at first sight.

References

Appleby, Joyce, Lynn Hunt, and Margaret Jacob
   1994 *Telling the Truth about History*, London and New York: Norton.
Banks, Diane
   2006 *Writing the History of Israel*, London: T&T Clark.

Elton, G. R.
   2002   *The Practice of History*, 2nd ed., Oxford: Blackwell.
Frei, Hans W.
   1974   *The Eclipse of Biblical Narrative: A Study in Eighteenth- and Nineteenth-Century Hermeneutics*, New Haven and London: Yale University Press.
Fulbrook, Mary
   2002   *Historical Theory*, London: Routledge.
Keller, Werner H.
   1956   *The Bible as History*, London: Hodder (rev. ed., 1980).
Moore, Megan Bishop
   2006   *Philosophy and Practice in Writing a History of Ancient Israel*, London: T&T Clark.
White, Hayden
   1973   *Metahistory: The Historical Imagination in Nineteenth-Century Europe*, Baltimore: Johns Hopkins University Press.
Whitelam, Keith W.
   1996   *The Invention of Ancient Israel: The Silencing of Palestinian History*, London and New York: Routledge.

Part One

Resources

Chapter Two

Bible I

Chronology, Facts, and Causality

One of the first tasks facing the biblical historian is to ask, and try to understand, what kinds of interests the ancient writers of our biblical texts took in their past. How did they consider the things that we regard as backbones of modern history writing: chronology, facts, and causal explanation? What did these authors know about the past, what did they care about the past, and why did they write at all about the past (this last question is as important as the others)? Before plundering their stories for history we need to appreciate the stories as they have been left, as clues to the attitudes and circumstances that generated them.

The biblical writers unfortunately did not tell even their original readers why they wrote; moreover, we do not know who they were or when they wrote or for whom, or what their resources were. We can—and do—guess, or deduce what we can. But first we can look at their practice, at how they actually deal with what we now regard as the backbones of modern history writing.

Chronology

The Monarchs of Israel and Judah

I want to begin with a statement that on any criterion is erroneous (1 Sam. 13:1): "Saul was a year old when he began to reign, and

21

he reigned two years over Israel." This is what the canonical (Masoretic) Hebrew text says. Most surviving Greek manuscripts, which go back to the earliest translations made of the original Hebrew, omit this verse entirely; of those that do include it, some have "one year" and some "thirty years" for the first figure. The Syriac Peshitta (another fairly early translation of the Hebrew) has Saul's age as twenty-one and omits the second part of the verse. This evidence tells us that the statement in the Hebrew text is not a later textual error but predates the Greek translation, which either chose to omit it or correct it. Unfortunately, the four manuscripts of 1–2 Samuel from Qumran preserve between them something of every chapter of 1 Samuel except 13 and 22 (Abegg, Flint, and Ulrich, 1999). Among English translations, the King James Version renders the Hebrew accurately (one year old, reigned two years), while the Jewish Publication Society Bible (JPS), which generally follows the Masoretic text exactly, omits Saul's age. The New Revised Standard Version (NRSV) reads, "Saul was . . . years old when he began to reign; and he reigned . . . and two years over Israel," implying that something is defective with both figures. The Net Bible supplies thirty for the first figure and forty for the second.

To make matters more intriguing, there is also a New Testament figure in Acts 13, where Saul/Paul is described as saying that King Saul reigned for forty years. This may explain the New International Version's total of forty-two, inserting the forty from Acts before the two from 1 Samuel. But where does Acts get its figure of forty? Apparently not from the Hebrew or Greek versions of 1 Samuel, so perhaps from the figures given for the reigns of both David and Solomon (forty years each). But was that forty years meant, or understood, to be an exact figure, or as an approximation—perhaps meaning a generation?

There is surely enough here to provoke our curiosity about regnal dates. The author(s) of 2 Kings (and Chronicles) enumerate the lengths of reign (and sometime age of accession) of every king and so appear concerned to provide an overall chronology for the monarchic era. Additionally, 2 Kings furnishes synchronisms between the rulers of Judah and Israel. The presence of approximate or incorrect figures would undermine the entire exercise. But it has always been clear to any attentive reader that the figures in the books of Kings contain what William Barnes has called "inconsistencies and outright contradictions" (Barnes 1991, 2; for a full enumeration of the discrepancies, see Thiele 1951). Both Barnes and Galil (1996) provide useful reviews of previous research as well as their own solutions. As examples of such discrepancies and contradictions, Barnes offers the case of Amaziah of Judah who began to reign in the second year of Joash of Israel, and reigned for twenty-nine years (2 Kgs. 14:1–2). But we are also told that Joash reigned sixteen years (2 Kgs. 13:10), and was succeeded by Jeroboam II, who reigned for forty-one years (2 Kgs. 14:23). Hence Jeroboam will have come to throne in Amaziah's fifteenth year—as 2 Kings 14:23 calculates. But Amaziah's son Azariah/Uzziah came to the throne in Jeroboam's twenty-seventh year (2 Kgs. 15:10). This leaves a gap of twelve years (Jeroboam's fifteenth to twenty-seventh years) during which time no one apparently ruled in Judah.

Again, Zimri is said to have reigned for seven days only, beginning in the twenty-seventh year of Asa of Judah (2 Kgs. 16:15–29). But his successor, Omri, began in Asa's thirty-first year. If we now bring in external evidence and correlate the biblical data with Assyrian and Babylonian king lists we find several discrepancies, such as (again, the example is from Barnes), the accession of Hezekiah. According to 2 Kings 18, his reign began before the fall of Samaria (721 BCE), but Sennacherib's invasion of Judah (701) is dated by his own account to Hezekiah's fourteenth year, implying that he was not on the throne until several years later.

In fact, the total biblical figure for the kings of Judah (but not Israel) is higher than those we can nowadays accurately reconstruct from events described by both biblical and Assyrian sources. A frequent solution has therefore been to infer periods of co-regency between some monarchs and their successors; in addition, a system (in Judah, at any rate) of postdating is often proposed, in which the monarch's accession year is counted as a full year. Finally, differences between the date of the new year in Judahite and Mesopotamian calendars can be cited to account for differences of single years. Galil employs all of these explanations; on the other hand, Hayes and Hooker (1988) deny wholly or partly all of these in proposing a different explanation. Now, postulating co-regencies is a simple and easy solution. Whenever there is a discrepancy, one assumes a co-regency of the requisite number of years! But are co-regencies mentioned in 2 Kings? One interesting case is Jehoram and Jehoshaphat. The Hebrew text of 2 Kings 8:16 reads: "In the fifth year of King Joram son of Ahab of Israel and Jehoshaphat king of Judah, Joram son of King Jehoshaphat of Judah began to reign. . . ." But this is a very odd formulation (if not as odd as Saul being a year old on accession), and both the NRSV and JPS amend it, while the phrase "and Jehoshaphat king of Judah" is absent from the Greek text (and so from some ancient Hebrew ones). A more plausible co-regency is between Azariah and his son Jotham (2 Kgs. 15:5). Since Azariah (who is, strangely, later called Uzziah) contracted leprosy, "Jotham the king's son was in charge of the palace, judging the people of the land." But the writer does say he "ruled," and the statement in verse 32 that "in the second year of king Pekah son of Remaliah of Israel, king Jotham son of Uzziah of Judah began to reign" dates from Uzziah's death, not his leprosy (as can be worked out from the correlations with the kings of Israel). There really is no ground for assuming co-regency. W. F. Albright (as cited in Galil 1996, 4–5), who was generally very conservative in adhering to biblical data, was perhaps right in concluding from his own examination of the figures that the chronology in Kings does not go back to original sources but entails a good deal of creativity.

In this verdict, Albright, unusually for him, comes close to the conclusion of Julius Wellhausen, that the figures do make sense exactly as they are, but that the sense is schematic. To see this we have to note that the biblical chronology of which these reigns are part gives a total of 430 years from the foundation of the temple to its destruction.

Now, 430 years is also the figure given in Exodus 12:40 for the sojourn in Egypt. But if we add 50 (exilic) years, we reach a total of 480 between the construction of the First and Second Temples. This, the product of the numbers 12 and 40, is the same figure as 1 Kings 6:1 gives for the period between the exodus and the building of the temple. According to the biblical chronology of Exodus, that is also the year in which the tabernacle, the protoype of the temple, was built. The Israelites took three months to reach Sinai from Egypt, which they left in the first month (Exod. 19:1). The tabernacle was then actually set up on the first day of the next year (Exod. 40:1).

One apparent problem with Wellhausen's calculation, however, is the 50 years allowed between the destruction of the First Temple and the building of the Second. More familiar to readers of the Bible is a figure for the exile of 70 years, as in Jeremiah 25:11–12; 29:10; Zechariah 7:5; and 2 Chronicles 36:21 (cf. Dan. 9:2). But should we assume that all parts of the Bible display the same chronological system? Presently we shall look at another one that can be expressed in both 70-year and 50- (or maybe 49-) year units. As for this chronological scheme, quite apart from the fact that from the fall of Jerusalem to Cyrus's conquest of Babylon is almost exactly that figure (586–539)—which is not really relevant and makes no argument in favor of a schematic figure—Ezra 1–3 puts the commencement of the building of the Second Temple in Cyrus's first year and thus may be working with a figure of 480 years from the building of the First Temple. The 50-year schema also happens to be in accordance with the jubilee law of Leviticus 25, according to which alienated land reverts to its original owner in the jubilee (49th or 50th) year. This law would mean that those exiled were entitled to have their Judean property restored from those to whom it had been given on their deportation after a period of 50 years.

So there seem to be two schemes, one including a 50-year and one a 70-year exilic era. In fact, they seem to have been combined in more than one place. According to Ezra 4:24, the immediate work on the temple ceased and was not resumed until the "second year of Darius," which would be 521 or maybe 520. On this calculation, we have a 70-year interval, as in Zechariah 1:12; 7:5. The curious case of the twice-built Second Temple in Ezra may therefore be less a matter of historical than schematic chronology, the double building fulfilling two chronological schemas.

A further aspect of this double reckoning of the exilic period is in Leviticus 26:35 and 2 Chronicles 36:21. These texts comment that the removal of Judah's inhabitants by the Babylonians allowed the land to experience the sabbatical years it had not previously enjoyed. Leviticus does not give a figure, but Chronicles does: 70 years. This implies a total period of neglect of the land of about 70 times 7 (490), which is as close as one can get to reconciling a total based on 12 and 40 with one based on 7.

Now we can get to the point. The previous discussion is not playing with biblical figures: it is rather a case of taking biblical chronology very seriously, at face value, and on its own terms. The essential point is that looking for "correct" historical figures is what a modern historian would do. But the biblical figures, if individually credible (except for Saul), and even approximately right do not necessarily aim at a historically correct total but one that is correct in another sense. They add up in a way that for those who calculate them is more important. If any reader is still in doubt about this, another biblical chronology provides yet a further schema: "So all the generations from Abraham to David are fourteen generations; and from David to the deportation to Babylon, fourteen generations; and from the deportation to Babylon to the Messiah, fourteen generations" (Matt. 1:17).

So our Bible can accommodate more than one way of calculating the same era. Indeed, different texts may give us different figures—surely not attributable to careless or innumerate scribes, nor to corrections in the light of better knowledge. It has been argued (Shenkel 1968) that the figures of regnal years in the Septuagint may be more original than in the MT. This conclusion is disputed, and the Greek figures are not internally consistent either. But differences within and between editions of biblical writings imply tampering, which itself gives pause for thought. Is it the individual figures or the schemes that are being adjusted? Indeed, let's note, in passing, one further case of schematization, which casts some doubt not just on chronology. The books of Kings list twenty kings after Solomon in each of the kingdoms of Israel and Judah. Now, the kingdom of Judah lasted over a century longer than Israel, which makes this equivalence very curious, not to say suspicious. Admittedly, more of the Israelite kings died prematurely (Zechariah, Shallum, and Menahem, for instance, all reigned during a single year: see 2 Kgs. 15)—but is this a historical fact, or a striking example of how the numbers were manipulated? Moreover, standing in eighth place in each series is a wicked woman: Jezebel and Athaliah (see Auld 2007).

The total of 430 years for the First Temple may have been arrived at with the aid of figures correctly gathered from official records. But it is also made up of reigns of 40 years assigned to David and Solomon (1 Kgs. 2:11; 11:42), which must contribute to the exact total and so have to be taken literally and not as approximations. Nor must we forget the two years that Saul ruled. The statement that he was a year old when he began to reign is a problem of fact, but if we alter the figure we will alter the correct total. Which is more important? I hope the reader is not already tired of arithmetic: we have to do some more to make the case that biblical chronologies are usually (if not always) schematic.

Before the Monarchs, and After

The biblical chronology from Adam to the exodus is as precisely stated as it is for the kings of Israel and Judah—and a further similarity is that the Hebrew, Greek, and Samaritan figures again do not exactly agree. For every ancestor from Adam to Terah, we get a formula that is a fairly precise equivalent of the monarchic one. Here, however, the age of each patriarch's begetting of his primary descendant is given—the equivalent of age of royal accession. In both cases, such information permits—even encourages—us to consider the total that can be reached as significant. The similarity in the formulation of the data, which are found in Genesis 5; 9:28–29; and 11:10–26, 32, betrays, as with the formulae in Kings, a single scheme. This scheme is attributed by most scholars to the priestly writer (there is a markedly variant genealogy, attributed to the Yahwist, from Cain to Noah in Gen. 4:17–24 with a fragment in 5:28). And again, as in the Messianic genealogy of Matthew 1, we find a generational pattern: ten generations span Adam to Terah and a further ten span Noah to Abraham (in the Greek text ten generations bring us to Terah; an extra ancestor, Kenan, has been imported). Chronological reckoning continues into Exodus, but without the formulae. Here we meet a major inconsistency: while the Egyptian sojourn is assigned 430 years (Exod. 12:40), the genealogy in Exodus 6:14–25 provides only four generations from Levi to Moses. What is extremely interesting is that two different calculations also crop up together in Genesis 15. In foretelling the fate of Abraham's descendants, Yahweh says in verse 13 that they will be oppressed in a foreign land for 400 years, while in verse 16, it is predicted that they will return to the land "in the fourth generation." These sets of alternatives cannot be matched exactly, but the number 4 seems to play an important part in all of them.

What, unfortunately, we cannot do with as much probability as we can with the monarchies is reconstruct what may have been the original chronological scheme that produces such figures for the period before the exodus. Several efforts have been made; the most thorough is probably by Hughes (1990), who has made a plausible effort to reconstruct an original system that sets the birth of Abraham 1,600 years after the creation. But as with other calculations noted earlier we are frustrated by variation and internal inconsistency.

It is easier to tackle the possible scheme for this era if we look more broadly at the phenomenon of Jewish chronological reckoning and then try to fit this period into it. The most explicit biblical chronological schema is in Daniel. Daniel's system only covers the exilic period onward, and, as is well known, chapter 2 utilizes a system of successive ages represented by the metals gold, bronze, and iron, and then iron and clay mixed, a system thought to be borrowed from Hesiod. But a more precise scheme emerges in chapter 9, where the 70 years of exile given in Jeremiah is interpreted to mean 70 "weeks of years," namely 490 years. We find similar systems of reckoning in other Jewish works of about the same period, writings that are not in most modern Bibles but were very probably scriptural for some Jews, as their presence and influence among the Dead Sea Scrolls seems to suggest. The Apocalypse of Weeks in 1 Enoch (93:1–10; 91:11–17) divides all history into ten weeks, beginning with creation. The weeks, however, seem to be of uneven length and the most significant ones usually happen at the end of the week, so it seems that the delimitation of the weeks was determined not by a fixed period but by epochs culminating in climactic events—as with the construction and destruction of the Jewish Temples, as we saw earlier. The Apocalypse of Weeks itself reflects a standpoint in the seventh week, with the divine judgment beginning in the eighth. After the judgment is completed in the tenth week, there will be an eternity of righteousness. The Melchizedek midrash from Qumran Cave 4 also divides its history into ten periods—this time, jubilees—at the end of which comes the great Day of Atonement in which the heavenly high priest Melchizedek will bring to an end the period of Israel's sin. This scheme is remarkably like Daniel's, with the same total (490 years), though divided differently. Although the text does not make it clear, the periodization probably also starts at the exile.

These calendrical calculations are often thought to have been stimulated by the crisis under Antiochus IV in which the Jerusalem cult of Yahweh was replaced by, or converted into, a cult of Zeus and the daily sacrifice for sin ceased. The expectation of an imminent end to this trauma was reinforced in some cases by an appeal to a divine plan for history that utilized a schematic calendar. The historical review in Daniel 9 and 10–12 clearly identifies the Antiochean measures as the final crisis. But the Apocalypse of Weeks does not betray any awareness of these events, and calendrical calculation was already an established feature of Jewish speculation about history. Disagreements about the "true" calendar may also be involved here: 1 Enoch celebrates a calendar based on the solar cycle, with a 364-day year divided into 12 months of 30 days. The book of Jubilees, written in the late second or early first century BCE, employs the same calendar, and rehearses the events from creation to Sinai, dividing time into weeks and jubilees and demonstrating that the patriarchs were aware of the Sinai laws even before they were revealed to Moses. Thus, for example, they never make a journey on a Sabbath (which, because of the regular total of days in a year, always fall on the same dates every year). Daniel, which does not indicate any calendrical preference, nevertheless refers to the importance of such issues for Jews by describing the "little horn" as "changing the sacred seasons and the law" (Dan. 7:25). Just as the week, the month, and the year were regarded as divinely ordained, built into the fabric of creation (see Gen. 1), so it was felt that history also was subject to such divisions. These examples perhaps explain more clearly the importance of such schemes in other biblical books. Time, like space, is sacred and meaningful and reflects the divine will and order.

These writings belong to the Hellenistic period (third century BCE onward), and they are sometimes called "postbiblical"— except for Daniel, which *is* a biblical book. Is there any continuity between the chronologies of the Pentateuch and Kings and the chronologies of these works? Let's return to the chronology of the Masoretic text, which we can abbreviate as follows (the following table is from Thompson 1999, 73–75):

Flood	1656 (years after creation)
Abraham's birth	1946/8
Exodus	2666
Building of First Temple	3146
Destruction of First Temple	3576
Edict of Cyrus/Building of Second Temple	3626 (allowing 50 years from the destruction of the First Temple)

We see immediately that between the birth of Abraham and the building of the First Temple is exactly 1,200 years. But more significant is that the exodus occurs at a point (2666) that is two-thirds of 4,000. By adding the remaining 375 years we arrive—in our modern calculations—at 538–375=163 BCE, the date of the rededication of the temple by Judas Maccabee. Of course, this calculation implies that the framers of the chronology were aware of the accurate figure, which is not necessarily the case. Daniel, as we have seen, supposes 490 years between the destruction of the First Temple and the restoration of the Second Temple after its defilement. (Many Jewish calculations of this period, such as that of Josephus, are also schematic.) So possibly 167 is the more important date, the year of desecration, or even a date a little in the future, the date of the eschaton, which so many Jewish writings of this period anticipate.

On this reconstruction, at any rate, we would expect the Samaritan Pentateuch to differ, since its chronology will obviously not feature the Jerusalem temple, and their system can be interpreted to reflect a calculation of the foundation of the Gerizim temple by Phinehas in 2800 AM (*Anno Mundi*). (Hughes, 238). The Septuagint chronologies, which provide longer periods for the lives of the pre-Abrahamic figures, are less transparent, but may presuppose a total of 5,000. We may, in any case, have to reckon with some interference of Christian calculation in the text of the Greek Bibles.

Even if the present Masoretic chronology dates from the second century BCE or later, that conclusion does not mean that earlier systems were not also applied; we have seen evidence that such calculations were indeed modified from time to time. The point of all the preceding discussion is this: if chronology is a backbone of our modern history, then it is also a backbone of the Bible's history—but in a different sense. Biblical dates and periods tend to be symbolic. The modern historian cannot—and indeed should not—use biblical chronology as a starting point for calculating precise dates. This is true of individual dates as well as of longer durations: the lifespans of the antediluvian ancestors are just as precise as those of the Israelite and Judean kings. We should, in short, use biblical chronology in ways that respect its own purposes.

As a final example, let me take the story of the flood in Genesis 6–9. Here are traces of two different chronological schemes. One gives absolute dates, the other intervals. The absolute dates integrate with a wider genealogical scheme in Genesis: Genesis 7:6 has Noah entering the ark at the age of 600: verse 11 has the deluge commencing on the seventeenth day of the second month of his life; on the seventeenth of the seventh month the ark comes to rest on the "mountains (plural!) of Ararat" (8:4) and on the first day of his 601st year the waters dry up; on the twenty-seventh of the second month he is commanded to leave the ark (8:13–19). We are also told that the inundation lasted 150 days (7:24; 8:3) and so we can calculate that each month had 30 days. This is significant, since it correlates with the calendar found in Enoch, Jubilees, and the Dead Sea Scrolls, but not the standard biblical calendar, which follows lunar months. Alongside this chronology is a much looser one in which we have 7 days between the divine command and the onset of the flood, and 40 days of rain (7:4). Later, Noah waits 7 days, then another 7 days, before leaving the ark (8:10, 12). The two schemes do not match. But they show us two different kinds of reckoning: in one, periods of time are represented by conventional numbers (7, 40: compare the reigns of David and Solomon); in another we have precise figures that measure long stretches of the past. Neither scheme is intended to be what we would call an accurate historical reckoning.

I hope the reader has been fascinated rather than wearied by the foregoing arithmetic. An even more systematic exploration of schematic chronological systems in the Bible has been done by Stenring (1965) and Larsson (1973), who conclude that the Pentateuch, the Deuteronomist, Jeremiah, Ezekiel, and the book of Chronicles were submitted, as a corpus, to a final redaction in the third century BCE by a group who imposed upon it an intricate chronological system. The point I want to insist upon is not that any one or other of the proposed chronological systems works (and most of them do, on their own terms, at least), but that there is a great deal of evidence of schematic chronological systems throughout the biblical narrative and that using the biblical data for a critical reconstruction of chronology is ill-advised. Our ancient authors did not deal with time in quite the way we do.

Facts

Kings or Chronicles?

"Facts," runs the saying, "are sacred," ergo, biblical facts especially so. Again, we have to be cautious and respectful in the way we convert biblical facts into modern facts. The past, for biblical writers, is indeed a source of knowledge, but that knowledge is not always what we would call factual.

Students of the Bible should know that the accounts of Judean history in the books of Kings and Chronicles are not identical. When very young, I failed to understand why it was necessary to have the same story told twice (though curiously I never regarded the Gospels in the same way). The original Christian term for the books is *paralipomena*, "things left out" (of Samuel and Kings)— not in fact a very accurate description, but an attempt, perhaps, to explain the presence of these books in the canon. There has been a lot of debate recently about how we moderns should understand the Chronicler—a theologian, a midrashist (interpreter of older texts), or a historian? The answer is that all three are reasonable answers. The common view is that the Chronicler, writing somewhere between the late fifth and early third centuries BCE, used the books of Kings as his source but embellished and altered certain details to fit his own ideological requirements. Thus, to use the best-known example, though Solomon actually had the temple built, the real founder, according to Chronicles, is David. Another is the Chronicler's story of Hezekiah's Passover, which 2 Kings 23:22 contradicts: it says of Josiah's Passover that no such Passover had been kept "since the days of the judges." Chronicles also omits David's domestic troubles, Saul's persecution, and everything about the kingdom of Israel after its secession from Jerusalem, but it adds that Israelites came to Hezekiah's Passover (2 Chron. 30:1–12). Kings, on the other hand, regards all the Israelites as having left the land (2 Kgs. 17). There are other minor discrepancies of fact and of judgment: the king known in 1 Kings as Abijam is called Abijah in Chronicles; in Kings he is a bad king, but in Chronicles a good one.

Of course the historian will want to decide which of these contradictory accounts is correct, or more correct (if that can be done). But most of these cannot be decided purely by comparing the texts. In any case, the prior task is understanding how such differences arise; that may in fact lead toward a preference for one of them.

The conventional scholarly view is that Chronicles is based on Kings, and was written two centuries or more later. If this is correct, the Chronicler is rewriting an existing work. In some places, perhaps, he has some historical sources not available to the writer of Kings, but these are hypothetical; by and large, he is changing data to suit his own way of looking at things, and doing so without any direct knowledge of what the data are based on—including any "facts." Why can this writer just change the content of his sources? Such a procedure is indeed irresponsible for a modern historian, but it was normal procedure for ancient historians, who had no direct access to the distant past, except for previous accounts. The existence of such accounts posed a problem: they had on the one hand to be (largely) followed, since they constituted an existing knowledge of the past. But they presumably had to be changed. In the first place, there is no point in copying slavishly an existing source. On the other hand, times, fashions, and of course patrons change, and the old story needs tweaking—but hardly for the sake of it, and certainly not changed because better knowledge had come to light. Any change to the story was necessary, surely, because for some reason a new account was required, which leads us to ask: What sort of requirements dictate a new account of the past? And, indeed, what is the function of *any* such story?

Another interesting question is: how will the later version stand alongside the earlier? The modern historical mentality can operate with different interpretations of the same facts, but not different sets of facts. Facts are either facts or not, and events either occur or do not. Biblical writing about the past does not appear to work on this principle. A story can be told in differing ways without, apparently, raising the question of whether the facts were really in accordance with one or other version. The presence of both Kings and Chronicles within the scriptural canon suggests that.

Chronicles is the one internal biblical example of a rewriting of the past—if we exclude 1 and 2 Maccabees, which may be independent accounts, or Daniel's rewriting of exile and (non)restoration. There are many other examples of the rewriting of biblical stories. One is the book of Jubilees (biblical, according to some canons); another is the huge work of Jewish history, the *Biblical Antiquities* of Flavius Josephus. Anyone reading his account of the history of Israel—a good deal longer than the scriptural one—will find additional detail, more conversation, richer motivation, and names for previously unnamed characters. Josephus, as a historian, feels entitled to make up details that render his account fuller and more interesting. Some of these details can also be found in other Jewish works of the period, and at times Josephus is clearly relying on retellings of the biblical stories already in circulation. Did he believe these versions to be authentic historical records, appropriate to be combined with the scriptural account? Or was he attempting to represent in his own words a story for which the biblical text was only the beginning, a kind of template or reference point? If so—and Josephus scholars are generally agreed that this was the case—he was not in this respect different from most other ancient historians of the classical era. He obviously had respect for the scriptural story but did not regard the biblical account as a sober and accurate version of the historical truth that must be dutifully preserved. It was *a story that could be manipulated.* The task of the historian of the distant past in Josephus's time was not to provide a better-researched account (hardly possible) but a more adequate understanding. And this understanding was achieved, of course, by telling the story differently.

Among the Qumran scrolls, we also find what has come to be referred to (among other terms) as "rewritten Bible." The contents of Genesis were especially prone to such treatment. The first of these to be discovered, and the best known, is the *Genesis Apocryphon.* It is written in Aramaic and preserved only partially. This is unfortunate, since it seems to be a sequence of pseudo-autobiographical anecdotes. At one point, the speaker/writer is Lamech, father of Noah; in another, Enoch, father of Methuselah, and later Abraham. Here is how Abraham tells the story of Sarai's recruitment into Pharaoh's harem (Gen. 12).

> When the king heard the words of Hyrcanus and his two companions, which they spoke unanimously, he desired her greatly and sent immediately for her. When he gazed on her he was struck by her beauty and took her as a wife. He wanted to kill me but Sarai said to the king, "He is my brother," so that I could benefit from her. I, Abram, was spared because of her, and was not killed. But I wept bitterly that night— both I and my nephew Lot, because Sarai had been forcibly

taken from me. That night I prayed, beseeched and begged, and spoke in sorrow as my tears ran, "Blessed are you, O God most high, my Lord, for ever. For you are lord and master of all and rule over all the kings of the world, to judge them all. Now I place my grievance before you, my Lord, against Pharaoh Zoan, King of Egypt, . . . during this night may he not be able to defile my wife. . . ."

This version of events claims, like a lot of Jewish writing of the period, to originate with an authoritative figure of the past, and on this basis can justify any deviation or amplification from the scriptural account. This account, among other features, salvages Sarah's virtue and insists on Abraham's concern for the fate of his wife, both left in doubt in the Genesis account. Other rewritings of the flood story are designed, like the book of Jubilees, to impose a certain calendrical scheme on the events (see above on the biblical chronology). From the second century CE we have the book of *Biblical Antiquities* that covers the biblical story from Adam to Saul. Then there are the Targums, paraphrases of the biblical text originating perhaps in synagogue liturgy but flourishing in the Middle Ages as literary texts that, because they were in Aramaic and not Hebrew, were not in danger of being confused with the biblical text they were paraphrasing.

This process of expansion and redefinition of history is paralleled in early Jewish law: the revelation at Sinai was supplemented by exegeses and applications, and even by additions that are all given Mosaic authority by being presented as revealed there and then to him. The Qumran Temple Scroll and, much more comprehensively, the Mishnah present themselves as Sinaitic law—though the inclusion of references to rabbis and their rulings in the Mishnah makes it clear that the Sinaitic origin of the Mishnah itself as oral law is not a historical claim, but means that everything in the Mishnah is logically entailed by the written law. And let us not forget that laws are even rewritten within the Pentateuch: the book of the Covenant (the *Mishpatim*) in Exodus 20:18–23:33 covers similar ground to Deuteronomy, but one is a rewriting or re-remembering of the other. Perhaps this analogy helps us to understand how biblical stories were understood: everything added or altered is in some way implied in the story itself, but not in the sense of "this is how it *must* have happened," but "here is another way in which it *could* have happened." We must acknowledge the fundamental distinction between a history that can only have happened one way (if we confine ourselves to the facts) and a story that permits various retellings. For the latter, our modern notion of history is appropriate and even impossible.

It is very difficult to specify the difference between all these texts: some are admittedly freer and more verbose than others, but they show how the biblical history was continually being rewritten. However, this is not a phenomenon that develops once a scriptural text has been established; they are not in that sense post-biblical. As is also true of law, we find exactly the same process of rewriting within the Bible itself—though obviously what is being rewritten did not at the time have biblical status. In the case of law, we can compare the book of the Covenant (the *Mishpatim*) in Exodus 20:18–23:33 with Deuteronomy.

But we now need to come back to Chronicles and Kings to make some further points. The modern scholarly consensus that Chronicles is dependent on Kings means that it is not to be valued so highly as a source. But there has always been an alternative view that the two accounts share a common source, and Graeme Auld (1994) has in fact reargued this view. The alternatives are not mutually exclusive. It has long been held that the Deuteronomistic History to which Kings is widely regarded as belonging underwent (at least) two editions, and Steven McKenzie (1991) has argued that Chronicles is derived only from the first edition (which he dates to the time of Josiah). This edition did not, he argues, include the cycle of prophetic legends associated with Elijah and Elisha. Much earlier, John Van Seters (1983, 277–91) had argued that the "court history" in 2 Samuel 9–20 and 1 Kings 1–2 was not "omitted" by the Chronicler but added into Kings later. Auld argues that Kings and Chronicles have both independently expanded their common source. So while we can still regard Chronicles as creative rewriting, the present biblical texts of Kings are too. The extent of midrash depends, of course, on how far their supplementary material was drawn from other sources and how far it was generated by way of expansive interpretation. The same phenomenon, in a more complicated form, is encountered in the case of the Synoptic Gospels: Mark is seen (by most scholars) as the source of both Matthew and Luke, whose expansions (again on the conventional scholarly view) include another source independent of Mark (Q) and the material unique to each. But among their unique material are their birth narratives, which are partly in agreement (Bethlehem birth, Nazareth residence, parental names, miraculous birth) but contradictory in others (reason for moving from Judah to Galilee, exact location of birth in Bethlehem), while Matthew's stories of Herod's massacre of the infants and of the magi and their star are widely suspected as creative legend and not as factual accounts. In all these cases, we find that because of the way ancient writers write about, and rewrite, the past, it is often impossible to tell the difference between what we would call history on the one hand and midrash, legend, or expansion on the other. Perhaps the distinction is our problem: perhaps for ancient readers the notion of what really happened is not crucial.

We can develop this line of inquiry by looking at episodes that are narrated in the Bible more than once but within the same storyline. Just as retellings of scriptural stories can lie happily alongside the original version without disturbing the notion of what really happened, so within the scriptural texts themselves, parallel accounts can lie side by side.

There is, for example, more than one account of the creation of humans and animals, how a patriarch's wife was passed off as his sister (Gen. 12; 20; 26), of how Saul was made king, how Saul and David met, how Daniel met Nebuchadnezzar, and how the Israelites gained possession (and how much) of the land of Canaan. We usually explain that these are signs of an editorial combination of originally independent versions of a single story. This may be true, but it does not explain how the ancient reader is supposed to understand past events. It is as if modern historians see things in traditional two-dimension representation, while biblical historians represent them as do cubist painters, who, having a flat canvas, paint an image from different perspectives. The result is quite different from a photograph. The picture makes no sense as a representation of what is seen in two dimensions, but it can represent more than one dimension within the frame of just two dimensions. Biblical storytellers are very happy to do the narrative equivalent of this; modern histories do not allow this dimension, unless they explicitly suggest alternative scenarios. But we are not talking about alternatives in the biblical accounts—not either-or, but both-and.

The examples show different ways of employing this device. The story of the patriarch's wife being passed off as his sister is not actually a threefold repetition of the same incident, even if it looks like the same story. The first occurrence involves Abraham and Sarah with the king of Egypt; the second Abraham and Sarah with Abimelech, king of Gerar; and the third Isaac and Rebekah—but again with Abimelech of Gerar. Twice the patriarch is the same, and twice the king, but the combination varies.

But Saul's choice as king is described in way that the modern historian could only regard as redundant. First (1 Sam. 9–10:16) he is chosen by divine prompting: Yahweh tells Samuel to await someone from Benjamin; for his part, Saul is sent to seek his father's donkeys and comes to a town that is unnamed but is probably meant to be Ramah, Samuel's home. On seeing Saul, Samuel hears a divine prompt that this is the man to anoint, which is done privately, outside the town. But then (10:16–11:14) a gathering of the tribes at Mizpah results in a lot-taking session, at which Benjamin, then the family of Kish, and then Saul are elected—although Saul has hidden himself and has to be discovered. The point of this double election is obviously that Saul was chosen by Yahweh and by the people—an important point to make. Reading this in the modern way we would conclude that this occurred in two distinct processes, though surely we would be troubled by the fact that a man already singled out and anointed should hide and have to be found when being elected by lot. We might also ask why the private anointing was even necessary if Yahweh was later going to choose him again by means of a lot. But if the ancient historian's technique is to tell the same story twice, these discrepancies have no significance. We may conclude, as most commentators do, that the narrator is drawing upon two stories of how Saul was chosen. But a modern historian would either choose the one that seemed more likely or would conflate them. This is obviously not what the ancient writer does; we get both versions consecutively. To ask what really happened is to mistake literal for symbolic significance.

The same phenomenon can also been seen in Saul's first encounter with David. Again, we have the private anointing by Samuel (surely to demonstrate that David had precisely the same qualifications as Saul), but then David meets Saul. But David's first introduction to Saul (1 Sam. 16:14–23) is when he is summoned to play the lyre to soothe Saul's "evil spirit." He is, however, depicted as "skillful in playing, a man of valor, a warrior, prudent in speech, and a man of good presence"—an ideal courtier, in fact. This portrait does not fit what we are told in the preceding anointing scene where he keeps the sheep for his elder brothers. Then in chapter 17 David meets Saul again, without either of them apparently knowing each other. Having defied Goliath's challenge, he is brought to the court. Now again he is depicted (and describes himself) as a humble shepherd boy, who feeds his father's sheep in between running errands for his elder brothers who are in Saul's retinue.

This part of the Goliath story (1 Sam. 17:12–31) is actually missing in the version of the story later translated into Greek. Was it omitted later, or added? We have at any rate another instance of conflicting portraits side by side without any apparent concern to integrate them into a single unambiguous account. Finally, in Daniel 1 and 2, Nebuchadnezzar is newly introduced to Daniel twice: in chapter 2 he is no longer the respected and consulted courtier of the king that he was in chapter 1 (Dan. 1:19–21) but an "unnamed Judean" of whose abilities the king has no idea (2:24–26).

There are many other cases where we have contradictory information: in 1 Samuel 14, Saul summons the ark to make an oracular inquiry. Recognizing the problem, the Greek text, and modern translation too, change "ark" into "ephod." But it's more likely that "ark" is a more original reading, since we can easily see how it might be altered to "ephod," but not how "ephod" might be altered to "ark." There are also contradictions about the status of Jerusalem. Here is what we are told:

The people of Judah could not drive out the Jebusites, the inhabitants of Jerusalem; so the Jebusites live with the people of Judah in Jerusalem to this day. (Josh. 15:63)

Zela, Haeleph, Jebus (that is, Jerusalem), Gibeah and Kiriath-jearim—fourteen towns with their villages. This is the inheritance of the tribe of Benjamin according to its families. (Josh. 18:28)

Then the people of Judah fought against Jerusalem and took it. They put it to the sword and set the city on fire. (Judg. 1:8)

But the Benjaminites did not drive out the Jebusites who lived in Jerusalem; so the Jebusites have lived in Jerusalem among the Benjaminites to this day. (Judg. 1:21)

David took the head of the Philistine and brought it to Jerusalem; but he put his armor in his tent. (1 Sam. 17:54)

The king and his men marched to Jerusalem against the Jebusites, the inhabitants of the land, who said to David, "You will not come in here, even the blind and the lame will turn you back"—thinking, "David cannot come in here." (2 Sam. 5:6)

The biblical writers obviously have different ideas about how and when the city came to be Judean and indeed whether it belonged to Judah or Benjamin. Of course, explanations for these and the numerous other discrepancies that could be listed can be given by assigning them to different periods or editors. But that is not my point. What matters is that these things are allowed to stand in the text without resolution. The discrepancies either were not noticed (which seems unlikely) or were not bothered about. Either way, we learn something about the extent to which biblical historians are punctilious about facts. They are not—at least not in the way we are. Contradictions are allowed to stand, details are embellished without any basis in historical knowledge. Are these writers bad or careless historians, or are we reading them wrongly and failing to share their understanding of the past?

Causality

The third and final backbone of modern history writing is causality: explanation of how and why things happen. From the ninth century BCE onward, the Assyrians embarked on an expansion policy that led them toward the Mediterranean and threatened the kingdoms of Syria and Palestine. Israel was drawn into resisting this advance, but ended paying tribute and, after withholding it (effectively rebelling), was dismantled and reorganized into three Assyrian provinces. Judah was at first an ally of Assyria (which undoubtedly did not come free), and after a rebellion by Hezekiah that was punished by the destruction of most of the country, with Jerusalem and little else left, the kingdom was returned to obedient subjection and, under Manasseh, even willing subjection. This account of the facts is based on what the books of Kings tell us, what the Assyrian records tell us, and what archaeology tells us. The modern historian will immediately seek to explain as well as report this. Thus, for example, Assyria was poor in manpower and natural resources as well as landlocked. Its expansion was dictated partly by economic considerations. Its military superiority, which was partly a result of its political organization, explains its success. Sennacherib's devastation of Judah came about because Assyria was stronger. Jerusalem was spared—well, here we have an interesting question. The likely explanation is that the king was bought off with a huge payment, and as a result abandoned the siege because his objective—submission—had been achieved. Possibly he was also only too happy to return home. The reasons for Hezekiah's rebellion probably involve the hope of assistance from Egypt, or perhaps a gamble on Assyria's distraction by resistance elsewhere.

The writers in the Bible have quite different notions of causality. They are uninterested in economic factors or *Realpolitik*, though surely they were not entirely ignorant of these. They are uninterested, indeed, in human motivation. But they do believe that history has a global explanation: what happens is what God determines. This is not peculiar to biblical historians. Most ancient historians also accepted this, including Herodotus, though his gods were capricious. Thucydides was exceptional in denying divine causality. But in the biblical scheme only one god is involved, and this makes it unique for its time. History cannot be explained by conflicts between different gods, which was a common explanation for other ancient historians. But the god in question was both a national and a universal one. The Assyrians (or at least their rulers) came quite close to this idea, as did the Achaemenid rulers of Persia. But they did not express it as clearly and did not leave us any bibles or any history writing, and so we cannot say that the biblical understanding of history was not unique. So, in the Bible, the history of Israel and Judah (which the biblical historians represent as a single nation) is not just part of universal history but the focus of it. When Assyria destroys Israel, when Babylonia invades Judah and deports the ruling dynasty and its supporters, the reason is that Israel and Judah have offended their deity; and this deity, with universal sovereignty, can use other nations to punish them. Military superiority, territorial ambition, the usual pattern of relations between kings and kingdoms, are of no consequence. This does not mean that these agents are innocent: despite obeying divine prompting, they nevertheless receive rebuke, and threat of divine punishment in their turn. That is human nature.

Similarly, when the families of humanity spread across the world and develop different languages, it is either because of a divine act (the collapsing of the tower and city of Babel/Babylon) or just a matter of course (Gen. 10). When Terah leaves Ur, he has no reason; when he goes to Canaan, it is not because he needs to leave Haran and find his own place, but simply because he is told to by his god. The cause of nearly all things is divine initiative, and if there is little curiosity about most events, it is probably because no answer is sought or imagined in terms of social, political, or economic motivation. Indeed, human motivation is not as commonly portrayed as we might nowadays expect of our historians. It is not that such immediate causes are always disregarded: when the patriarchs go from time to time to Egypt, they do so because of famine, a regular fear of the population of Palestine, something that influenced a great many of their actions (and prayers). But famines were caused by divine action (see Amos 4:6). The point is not that we should expect a prescientific culture to understand disease, economics, meteorology, or any of our modern explanations, but we should not forget that in respect of the third backbone of history, causality, biblical writers had a very different worldview from ours.

So when the account in 2 Kings 19 of Sennacherib's siege of Jerusalem reports that the king consulted the prophet Isaiah, who told him that God would "put a spirit" in the Assyrian king so that he would hear a rumor causing him to return to his land, and then "cause him to fall by the sword" there, and that later an "angel of the LORD" slew 185,000 of the Assyrian besiegers, we are unsatisfied; these comments do not allow us to understand what really happened. When modern historians are generally inclined to accept the basic facts of such a biblical account, they replace the biblical explanations with their own. Thus, for instance, Sennacherib had to leave hurriedly to quash a rebellion, or mice gnawed through the leather of the Assyrian armor. But preserving the facts (whether legitimately or not) while jettisoning the explanation damages the integrity of the biblical account: we cannot that easily siphon off the explanation and retain the fact. If we think we can, let us try it with the book of Judith. It describes events supposed to have taken place in the twelfth year under "Nebuchadnezzar, who ruled over the Assyrians" (1:1). But the Judeans have just returned from exile (4:3), and the land and people threatened are in Judea, but the usual term for them is "Israel." It has been suggested that the story is deliberately set in an impossible context. Or did the writers and readers have a very confused knowledge of their own past?

In much of what I have described in this chapter, the ancient Judean writers are in accord with the conventions of their time. In the Greek and its derived Latin historiography we can see, as well as the beginnings of questioning of sources and of comparison of accounts, a gradual waning of deference to divine motivation and a concentration on human causation. But we nearly always find an embedded morality. If in other respects the biblical historiography is less critically developed, it is one and the same with its insistence that if history does not teach something—and that means something to the present and something for the future—it is not worth doing.

Summary

There has been well over a century of often heated and sometimes overheated debate about whether the writing about the past in the Bible is history or myth, and whether we should trust it or doubt it. I deal in later chapters with these issues in terms of a historian's practice. Here I have wanted to show that we first have to understand it. Once understood, it becomes neither right nor wrong, neither good nor bad, and neither to be trusted or doubted; these verdicts all arise from imposing our criteria on it. Where matters of chronology, fact, and causation/explanation are concerned, the Bible shows every bit as much concern as we modern historians do, but its concern is with different things. The meanings they sought, and drew, in the past were for them probably more important than those we now try to draw ourselves.

References

Abegg, Martin, Peter Flint, and Eugene Ulrich
    1999   *The Dead Sea Scrolls Bible*, San Francisco: HarperSanFrancisco.
Auld, A. Graeme
    1994   *Kings without Privilege: David and Moses in the Story of the Bible's Kings*, Edinburgh: T&T Clark.
    2007   "Reading Kings on the Divided Monarchy: What Sort of Narrative?" in H. G. M. Williamson (ed.), *Understanding the History of Ancient Israel*, Oxford: Oxford University Press, 337–43.
Barnes, William Hamilton
    1991   *Studies in the Chronology of the Divided Monarchy of Israel*, Atlanta: Scholars Press.

Galil, Gershon
   1966   *The Chronology of the Kings of Israel and Judah*, Leiden: Brill.

Hayes, John H., and Paul K. Hooker
   1988   *A New Chronology for the Kings of Israel and Judah and Its Implications for Biblical History and Literature*, Atlanta: John Knox Press.

Hughes, Jeremy
   1990   *Secrets of the Times: Myth and History in Biblical Chronology*, Sheffield: JSOT Press.

Larsson, Gerhard
   1973   *The Secret System: A Study in the Chronology of the Old Testament*, Leiden: Brill.

   2002   "The Chronology of the Kings of Israel and Judah as a System," *Zeitschrift für die alttestamentliche Wissenschaft* 4: 224–35.

McKenzie, Steven L.
   1991   *The Trouble with Kings: The Composition of the Book of Kings in the Deuteronomistic History*, Leiden: Brill.

Shenkel, J. D.
   1968   *Chronology and Recensional Development in the Greek Text of Kings*, Cambridge, Mass.: Harvard University Press.

Stenring, K.
   1965   *The Enclosed Garden*, Stockholm: Almqvist and Wiksell.

Thiele, Edwin B.
   1951   *The Mysterious Numbers of the Hebrew Kings*, Chicago: University of Chicago Press (rev. ed., Grand Rapids: Kregel, 1994).

Thompson, Thomas L.
   1991   *The Mythic Past: Biblical Archaeology and the Myth of Israel*, New York: Basic Books.

Van Seters, John
   1983   *In Searh of History: Historiography in the Ancient World and the Origins of Biblical History*, New Haven: Yale University Press.

Chapter Three

Bible II

"Israel"

Having looked at some aspects of how the Bible writes about the past, we need to consider in a broader perspective the subject of its narratives: Israel (I have recently written a detailed treatment of the subject of this chapter [2007]). But first we must consider the structure and scope of the entire narrative.

First and Second Histories

There are two large-scale narratives about Israel. From Genesis to 2 Kings runs a single consecutive account from creation to the end of the kingdom of Judah. Biblical scholars do not regard this narrative as the work of a single writer or editor, or even as a single work. Rather, one account runs from creation to the death of Moses (represented now by Genesis–Numbers) and another begins with the end of Moses' career and ends with the deportation to Babylonia. The link between the two accounts is the book of Deuteronomy. According to the model proposed by Martin Noth and still widely accepted (Noth 1981, 1972), Deuteronomy originally stood alone as a lawbook (represented by chaps. 12–26), but was later attached as a preface to another story that ran from the initial conquest of the land until its loss at the end of the kingdom of Judah. This second composition is referred to as the Deuteronomistic History because it shares much of the language and ideology of Deuteronomy. But Deuteronomy itself has also been joined to the other narrative in two ways: by prefacing it with a review of the exodus and wilderness wanderings, thus making the laws part of a speech of Moses at the end of his life. This setting provides a natural sequel to the other narrative, and by moving the stories surrounding Moses' death from that narrative to the end of Deuteronomy, a fairly smooth link between the two is effected. The canonical structure later superimposed on this combined narrative actually breaks the narrative unity by separating Genesis–Deuteronomy (Pentateuch, Torah) from Joshua–Kings (Former Prophets). Such a structuring is presumably due to the legal content of Deuteronomy, which associates it rather with Exodus–Numbers.

The composition of the two narratives themselves is more complicated and finds less agreement. The majority view is that the Pentateuch comprises several strands, while the Deuteronomistic History, according to Noth, was the unified work of a single editor or group of editors. Neither view has unanimous support. Obviously the modern historian has to take a view on the compositional history of both, and, crucially, on the date of the laws of Deuteronomy, which provide the fulcrum for dating all the rest. But for the moment, the task is to read the entire narrative, fashionably referred to as the "Primary History" (or, as I prefer, "First History").

The second narrative begins with the books of Chronicles, which also takes the story from creation (strictly speaking, the creation of Adam) to the eve of the return of descendants of the deportees from Babylonia. Everything up to the death of Saul is recast in a summary form, and almost entirely genealogical. The narrative proper begins only in chapter 10 with Saul's final battle. The books of Ezra and Nehemiah (even Esther) are often added to the books of Chronicles to constitute the "Secondary History" (I prefer 'Second History," because this term does not imply any priority in terms of prestige, date, or accuracy). The legitimacy of this reading is debatable. In favor of linking at least Chronicles, Ezra, and Nehemiah is that the last verse of 2 Chronicles is also the first verse of Ezra, while in the Jewish Scriptures Ezra and

Nehemiah form a single book. They also form a sequence in the Christian canon (following the earliest Greek Bibles). Until the end of the twentieth century it was also the scholarly consensus that the three books were written by the same author. Against such a view is that in the Jewish Scriptures Chronicles is placed immediately after Ezra–Nehemiah, and that in the last few decades it has been widely thought that they did not share the same authorship. Certainly, there are important differences in ideology and presentation (see below). There is little reason to add Esther. It has no narrative links (plot, place, time) with the other books despite its place in the Christian canonical sequence; one might as well on these grounds add the books of Maccabees, Judith, or Tobit, or, on different grounds, Daniel.

What is the relationship between Chronicles, Ezra–Nehemiah, the Pentateuch, and the Deuteronomistic History (the Jewish Former Prophets)? There is little disagreement between Chronicles and the Pentateuch, and it is usually assumed (with very good reason) that the author(s) knew a pentateuchal text, though not necessarily everything now in it (no Cain or his descendants, for example). So we might take it that Chronicles is an alternative sequel to the Pentateuch rather than an alternative to the Pentateuch itself, since it does not replicate the pentateuchal narrative. As for Joshua–Kings, we have no parallel at all to the stories of Joshua, Judges, or 1 Samuel except the very last chapter. The Chronicler seems uninterested in what transpired before the time of David. From that point, his narrative follows quite closely, and often verbatim, the text of Samuel and Kings, though with interesting deviations. Nothing is recorded of events in the kingdom of Israel, and nothing of the events narrated in 2 Samuel 9–20 and 1 Kings 1–2, which deal with private matters in David's court. There are other deviations, too: King Abijam, who is criticized in Kings, becomes the good King Abijah; 2 Chronicles 20 has no parallel in Kings, and Manasseh spends time in Babylon where he learns to repent.

The scholarly consensus has been for some time that Chronicles rewrites 2 Samuel–Kings. The problem with demonstrating this assertion is that we cannot legitimately compare the two Hebrew texts as they have been handed down and because we have very good evidence that the text of Kings has been revised. The slightly different, more cautious view taken in the last chapter is that Chronicles and Kings both derive from the same source, which they sometimes repeat verbatim and sometimes alter. But whatever the truth, Chronicles needs to be taken seriously as an alternative account because its differences from Kings are very significant. This is also true in the case of Chronicles compared with Ezra–Nehemiah.

Fluctuating Biblical Israels

In this chapter we do not need to be concerned with any of these historical-literary-critical issues. We are interested only in the narratives themselves. From these we will able to show that "Israel" is a very variable entity, and that we cannot speak of a "biblical Israel" at all, only biblical Israels. Let's begin with the broad differences. From Genesis to Samuel, Israel is composed of twelve tribes, all descended from Jacob, who, being renamed "Israel" himself, gives rise to the "children of Israel." The tribes remain tightly united as a family, then a nation, until they have settled in Palestine. After the death of Joshua, they begin to act separately, though the corporate framework is still in place. There is a rupture of this fraternity at the end of Judges when the other tribes make war on Benjamin.

At this point, an unexplained shift occurs. The figure of Samuel is presented as a judge, but the territory over which he judges is restricted to the land of Benjamin (yes, the defeated tribe). He anoints Saul, a Benjaminite, whose kingdom seems not to extend over the twelve tribes but only a few. And he does not rule over Judah. For there is already a house of Judah, and this house will anoint David as its king. From this point onward until the end of 2 Kings, Judah is not regarded as Israel. Under David and Solomon the two houses are united, but not as a single Israel. Indeed, there is bitter rivalry between the families of David and Saul, and Saul's family is eventually wiped out. Judah is not referred to as being part of Israel—with two exceptions. One is 1 Kings 8, where Solomon gathers all "the elders of Israel" in Jerusalem. The second place is

2 Kings 17:18, where Judah is said to be the last remaining tribe of Israel (see further below). But in every other occurrence, "people of Israel" is either explicitly alongside "people of Judah," or the context suggests it does not include Judah. We should pay attention to this ambiguity very carefully.

Israel, according to 2 Kings 17, vanishes under the Assyrians. The inhabitants are transported, being replaced by foreigners who have to be taught the cult of the god of Israel, Yahweh. They partly follow this cult and partly maintain their own cults. But they are no longer Israel or even part of it. Verse 18 then says that only Judah is left of the tribes of Israel; the remaining tribes are deemed to have been lost, though other biblical texts hope for their return, and the tale of Tobit, who comes from the tribe of Naphtali, is set among these exiles. For the books of Kings, the history of Israel continues only through Judah, and indeed only through a Judah in exile. Although we are told "Judah went into exile out of its land" (2 Kgs. 25:21), there were "people who remained in the land of Judah" who were governed (or ruled) by Gedaliah. After his assassination, "all the people, high and low . . . went to Egypt" (v. 26). The statement is rather coy about whether these remainder are really Judah (Gedaliah actually seems to have been from Benjamin), but the ambiguity is finally made irrelevant, leaving only the question of whether those who fled to Egypt still belonged to Israel. The view of Kings is that the land was empty after this; the only Israel left was Judah, exiled in Babylonia: the Israel of the north had been scattered among the nations to which the Assyrians had taken them and it no longer counted.

One other curiosity remains in all this. When the ten tribes of the house of Israel rebel against Rehoboam, one tribe sides with Judah: Benjamin. This is mentioned in passing, but raises some significant questions. Of all the tribes inimical to Judah, Benjamin was the most hostile, according to the books of Samuel, which also present it as the tribe of the first Israelite king. The association of Benjamin with Judah is therefore remarkable, and even more so since unexplained. Just like the mysterious appearance of a house of Judah separate from the house of Israel is totally unprepared in the narrative, so is this. The enumeration of tribes—an essential feature of the pentateuchal Israel but too complicated to go into here in any detail—also creates a problem at this point (1 Kgs. 11:31–32):

> [Ahijah] then said to Jeroboam: Take for yourself ten pieces; for thus says the LORD, the God of Israel, "See, I am about to tear the kingdom from the hand of Solomon, and will give you ten tribes. One tribe will remain his, for the sake of my servant David and for the sake of Jerusalem, the city that I have chosen out of all the tribes of Israel."

This makes eleven tribes, no doubt. The notion of Judah as a single tribe also recurs in 2 Kings 17:18: "Therefore the LORD was very angry with Israel and removed them out of his sight; none was left but the tribe of Judah alone." Where is the missing tribe? Is it Levi, whose priests presumably divine among the two kingdoms? Or is it Benjamin, which was supposedly attached to Judah but is then disregarded? Does it matter? Yes, if the tribe is Benjamin, because while Judah is the name of the kingdom and the name of one of the tribes of Israel, the population of Judah is actually made up of three tribes: Judah, Levi, and Benjamin. We can add one more thing: at the end of 2 Kings, after the deportation of the Judean upper classes (or perhaps "all Judah"), the center of Judah moves to Mizpah, which is in Benjamin. We are not told (see below) when Jerusalem was reinstated as capital city, but it seems that for between 100 and 150 years Judah must have been ruled from Benjamin. Why is Benjamin so ignored then?

Chronicles has a dramatically different portrait of Israel and its components. From the time of Saul until the end of the kingdom of Judah there was only ever one nation that consisted of the twelve tribes—the Israel of Genesis to Judges—and in theory only one legitimate kingdom. The secession of the ten tribes was precisely that: an internal rebellion. Ten tribes abandoned the political regime appointed by the God of Israel, the line of David, and the city of Jerusalem. With the end of that kingdom, Israel was reunified (and celebrated by Hezekiah's Passover, an event unrecorded in Kings).

Another significant difference is in Chronicles' definition of Judah. It is quite clear that Judah includes Benjamin and Judah also. These are regularly enumerated. And indeed, Saul and his family are rather differently depicted as well. As already mentioned, the hostility between Saul and David is not featured in Chronicles. But there are also genealogies of Saul's family (1 Chron. 8:33–40; 9:39–44) that extend it well beyond the time of David. In fact, according to 8:28 many of them lived in Jerusalem. For Chronicles the presence of Benjamin within Judah is therefore important, while for Kings it is not.

Chronicles has, we might say, an inclusive Israel (like the Pentateuch), while Kings has an exclusive one, comprising only exiled Judeans. Instead of Judah alone, Chronicles includes Judah, Benjamin, and Levi within the kingdom of Judah, while the inhabitants of the northern kingdom are also part of Israel even after its disappearance. The claim in Kings that at the fall of Samaria these were removed and replaced is not recorded—but then, nothing is recorded of events in its history. The reason may be that the original source from which Chronicles and the present books of Kings derive had none of this information (it could have been added to Kings later), or the reason may be ideological: Chronicles did not regard this kingdom as a legitimately independent entity, but a missing part of its Israel. And certainly, Jerusalem, its temple and cult and the kingship of David (expressed also in his temple), is eternally the center of this twelve-tribe Israel.

This portrait of Israel becomes fuzzy when the kingdom of Judah ends, however. The view of Chronicles is clearer than Kings on one thing: the land was entirely emptied "until it had made up for its sabbaths," as it had not done while occupied by sinful Judah (2 Chron. 36:21). But what of Samaria, also part of Chronicles' Israel? Neither Kings nor Chronicles tells us what happened here when Jerusalem fell. For Kings their fate was irrelevant, since the province no longer belonged to Israelites. But according to Chronicles' presentation of Israel, Samaria belongs also to the land and its people to Israel. Hence it is not Israel that goes into exile, but only Judah. The story ends with the decree of Cyrus that the temple in Jerusalem may be rebuilt and the people return. The implication is therefore that the divinely chosen city and the tribes of Judah, Benjamin, and Levi will all be restored, and with it Israel in all its fullness.

The books of Ezra and Nehemiah (one book in the Jewish canon) continue the story, recapitulating the end of 2 Chronicles in Ezra 1:1. But although in many respects these books share the interests of Chronicles (note "Judah and Benjamin, and the priests and the Levites" in Ezra 1:5), they describe an outcome different from that apparently envisaged in Chronicles. Almost from the outset there is opposition to the rebuilding of Jerusalem and its temple from Judah's neighbors, including Samaria. The letter from their leaders to the Persian king Artaxerxes acknowledges that foreigners had been settled in Samaria, though it does not say that all Israelites had been deported. Nevertheless, the name "Israel" is exclusively applied not just to Judeans but to Judeans who had been deported and were returning. This definition of Israel is far from that of Chronicles, but close to, or identical with, that of Kings. Israel is now constituted only by a group of Judean immigrants, who claim to be the real heirs of the old kingdom, and the land, of Judah. Those who were in the land already are not regarded as Israel, but are called simply "people of the land." At the end of the book of Ezra, "foreign" wives are also "away." In Nehemiah, the governor of Samaria, Sanballat, opposes the rebuilding of the walls of Jerusalem, without success: later the people "separated from Israel all those of foreign descent" (Neh. 13:3).

Let's briefly list the various biblical Israels, from broadest to narrowest. The broadest is the Israel of twelve tribes. In Genesis, this Israel is a family, part of the Abrahamic clan and related to other Abrahamic families. It is part of a group including Aram, Moab, Ammon, Edom, and Ishmael. From Exodus onward this family becomes a nation and markedly more detached from even its Abrahamic neighbors. In Chronicles it becomes a single kingdom based in Jerusalem and constituting the whole territory of the kingdom of David, which in fact includes much of the land occupied by the Abrahamic nations. In the books of Samuel Israel seems to means territory—probably Benjamin, Ephraim, and Manasseh, the tribes descended, according to Genesis, from Rachel—ruled by Saul, but excluding Judah. In Kings Israel is used almost exclusively for the kingdom of the ten tribes, but at the end this kingdom no longer forms part of Israel, but only Judah. In Ezra and Nehemiah Israel is restricted not only to Judah but to those Judeans who returned from exile.

Which "Israel" Belongs in a Modern History?

What are the implications of this variety for modern historians? Two issues are raised. First, should we produce a biblical history of Israel? If so, can we responsibly only select one of them? If so, does that one include those who lived in the territory of the province of Samaria, who undoubtedly called themselves "Israel" too? Does it include the lost tribes whose membership of Israel is accepted by those texts that predict their return? Obviously, no one of these should be selected in preference to any others. Pretending that there is a clear biblical definition of Israel is, in any case, not just bad history, but bad theology and a poor and dishonest treatment of the Bible itself. The plurality, or flexibility, of biblical Israel is a biblical fact as well as a historical problem. Biblical Israels all need to be given a historical explanation. Indeed, although the Samaritans are not usually regarded as part of biblical Israel, they see themselves as Israel and share some of the same Scriptures as Judah. The Samarians (i.e., the former kingdom of Israel) from whom they derive are, as we have seen, not excluded from Israel in Chronicles, either. On what basis should they be excluded from a modern history?

The second issue is how, in accommodating all the various biblical Israels, a modern critical history can be constructed. What historical definition of Israel should the modern historian employ? In practice, where does one begin, where does one end, and whom does one include? Even if only biblical Israels are selected, it is obvious, even to most devoted adherents, that the Hebrew Bible is ultimately the product of Judeans and reflects Judean ideology. Must a modern history of Israel reflect only the ancient Judean point of view?

If the historian simply wants to present a true biblical history, then the answer is not to bother: that already exists and in an age of widespread literacy there seems no point in paraphrasing it. In this way the difficulties of harmonizing the various Israels into one are avoided. If, however, we do want to construct a history that conforms to modern principles of history writing and enables us to understand everything we can about the past, then we should address the different biblical Israels as reflecting different periods and viewpoints within the cultural history of communities that regarded themselves as Israel. The production of these definitions will have to be part of such a modern account. We shall also want to look at nonbiblical data in order to help us better judge how far any of these biblical Israels correspond to historical describable entities—historical Israels. For instance, the definition with which we are left by the books of Ezra and Nehemiah is a cul-de-sac, because we know from overwhelming amounts of other evidence that by the Greco-Roman period the majority of the population of Palestine, including Galilee and Edom/Idumea, was Jewish. Indeed, it might be argued that most of the territory between Egypt and the Euphrates was Jewish, in which case Abraham, not Jacob, is the more realistic ancestor of Israel. There are also strong doubts that the rift between Jerusalem and Samaria, which culminated in the destruction of the temple of Gerizim by the Judean king Hyrcanus in 126 BCE, goes back as far as the fifth century, where Ezra and Nehemiah are placed.

Summary

There is more than one story and within these stories more than one Israel. The historian needs to recognize the various profiles and consider how they might have arisen, and what interests and communities they might reflect. It is also, of course, necessary to discover which of these Israels, or which combination, best corresponds to our modern critical knowledge of the past. But to understand the biblical Israels in their own historical contexts we have to find our own historical Israel (or rather, Israel and Judah). How can we escape the circularity?

References

Davies, Philip R.
2007 *The Origins of Biblical Israel*, London: T&T Clark.

Noth, Martin
1972 *A History of Pentateuchal Traditions*, Englewood Cliffs, N.J.: Prentice-Hall (original 1948).

1981 *The Deuteronomistic History*, Sheffield: JSOT Press (original 1943).

Chapter Four

Archaeology
Use and Abuse

Beside the biblical texts themselves, historians have at their disposal the resources of archaeology. In the previous chapters we considered the ways in which biblical writers about the past carried out their tasks, and the problems that this posed for the modern historian. This chapter does the same for archaeology. Most archaeologists are not biblical critics, and most biblical critics are not archaeologists. Biblical historians need to be practitioners of both or at least well informed about both, and in particular, to be fully aware of how archaeology is carried out, and how it serves to solve historical questions.

Prof. Ze'ev Herzog, who heads the Institute of Archaeology at Tel Aviv University, recently declared (2007):

> There has been an important revolution in biblical history in the last decades. We are now uncovering the difference between myth and history, and between reality and ideology of the ancient authors. This is the role of our generation of archaeologists—to unearth the real historical reality to find out *why and how the biblical records were written.* (emphasis added)

Such a statement would probably seem to many readers of *Science Daily* quite unexceptional and even banal. But the existence of the Bible puts the archaeology of ancient Palestine into a special cat-

58

egory. It is not too much of a simplification to say that biblical archaeology has pursued three goals. The earliest was to illuminate the Bible. To fulfill this, the Bible's story of the past was taken for granted and remained only to be dramatized by recovered objects and places. Another early goal responded to scholarly claims that the Bible was not always reliable history; therefore it sought, as its practitioners often still say, to defend or prove the Bible against such attacks, as they were deemed. (These two goals are still pursued.) A third, more recent goal is defined by Herzog: to assist in finding out how and why the Bible was written. This goal has partly emerged as a result of the failure of the previous two goals. Large portions of the biblical story of the past cannot be either illuminated or defended by archaeology; they are either unverifiable or in many cases can be brought into serious doubt. They cannot be taken for granted even as rough drafts of history, but are clearly to some extent something else. This "something else" has to be understood, and archaeology can help, in two ways. It can—by showing in a clear and independent manner what data it has, what the data might mean, and (if asked) what history is consistent with the data—give us a (limited) template against which some of the biblical narratives might be assessed for their historical probability. It can also assist the historian in constructing a historical framework within which the production of the various stories, and their combination, might be assigned.

This task is for the present and the future. The modern historian needs to realize, however, just how ideologically driven biblical archaeology has been in the past, and regrettably still is in many quarters. Archaeology provides one of two major external sources of data about the past to which the Bible refers, and is therefore indispensable; but the data need interpreting intelligently, consistently, and with caution. Much of the accumulated archaeological data and their evaluation require revision.

I shall consider the historian's integration of archaeology and text in the next chapter. Here we are concerned with archaeology itself. The main lesson here is that just as the biblical text is a datum, but its meaning a matter of interpretation, so archaeological data also require interpretation. One of the pioneers of biblical archaeology, A. H. Sayce, observed, "We must not forget that in a fact of history or archaeology is included its interpretation by the archaeologist and the historian. The conclusion he draws is, in short, part of the fact itself" (1894, 556, quoted in Davis 2004, 25). Many archaeologists seem to have forgotten this rule, and it is worth bearing in mind.

Archaeology in Palestine has always been directed toward goals set by a biblical agenda, in its selection of sites, its concentration on a certain chronological era, and its interpretation of evidence. These all undermine the usefulness of biblical archaeology as a genuinely disinterested discipline, and a very brief review of its rise and fall will illustrate some of these goals.

The Rise and Fall of Biblical Archaeology

Western interest in the ancient Middle East (which for some reason is commonly referred to as the "ancient Near East") was born of politics and religion, as documented by Neil Asher Silberman (1982). Interest in the antiquities of this region is often traced back to Napoleon Bonaparte, who at the beginning of the nineteenth century brought with his armies to Egypt several surveyors, engineers, and scholars to study the country and its monuments. The Holy Land itself was first systematically explored a few decades later by the American clergyman Edward Robinson, whose motives were both scientific and religious. His travels were a mixture of survey and pilgrimage, and in 1841 and 1852 he published what he called his "Biblical Researches in Palestine." As Thomas Davis—whose excellent account I am largely following here—put it (2004, 10), Robinson was very much the "prototype biblical archaeologist," with a metaphorical spade in one hand and Bible in the other. Robinson's publications, together with the beginning of excavatory archaeology in Mesopotamia and Syria, led to the foundation of national societies devoted to studying Palestine. These pursued a mixture of ambitions. The British Palestine Exploration Fund was founded in 1865 by a group of distinguished academics and clergymen, and its agenda, though clearly influenced by biblical interests, professed to be scholarly; in contrast, the American

Palestine Exploration Society (PES), which lasted from 1870 to 1884, was explicitly devoted to illuminating and supporting the Bible in the face of the attacks on its historical reliability that had been accumulating during the nineteenth century. In 1870, the Society of Biblical Archaeology gave birth to the name of the new discipline, and its scope included not only Palestine but "other Biblical Lands." Henceforth, biblical archaeology could deal with any territory that fell within the range of the biblical histories—though not, as a rule, the classical world. The German Deutscher Palästina Verein was founded in 1877, and in its own words "united German language research on Palestine without any ties to politics or religious affiliations" (www.palaestina-verein.de/index.html).

In America, the demise of the PES was remedied by the founding of what came to be known as the American Schools of Oriental Research. Under the auspices of the Society of Biblical Literature and the American Oriental Society, a school was established in Jerusalem in 1900. ASOR was an officially secular institution, but biblical research has always been a major element in the schools' remit. For political reasons, the Jerusalem school was renamed the W. F. Albright Institute of Archaeological Research in 1970.

The balance of political, scholarly, and religious motives in biblical archaeology was never likely to sustain equilibrium. Polemics quickly developed. The literary-critical work of Julius Wellhausen was opposed, in the name of archaeology, by the British Assyriologist (and Anglican clergyman) A. H. Sayce. Sayce displayed what emerged as three main characteristics of biblical archaeology. First, he was no fundamentalist with a dogmatic belief in the infallible accuracy of Scripture; second, he contrasted the "facts" of archaeology to the "fancies of higher criticism" (i.e., the methods of Wellhausen and others); and third, he contrasted the scientific nature of archaeology to theology (Sayce was quoted earlier on the subjectivity of archaeological "facts"!)

This attitude was reinforced by wider political, social, and economic factors. While some archaeological expeditions have been carried out by national institutions—and increasingly have come under the overall supervision and control of national authorities—biblical archaeology is conducted not only by societies, universities, and seminaries but also private individuals (under license). It is often funded from sources with a religious (including Zionist) agenda. Institutions have their own reasons for archaeological work: science, academic prestige, and of course the acquisition of artifacts, while societies, often with political support, have promoted religious and imperial agendas as well as scientific ones. But several institutions sponsoring excavations in Palestine have been seminaries with denominational motives for "illuminating the Bible." Israeli archaeology was also for a long time motivated by a desire to illuminate the Jewish past and to encourage tourism, rather than to explore disinterestedly all aspects of the history of the land (the definitive account, richly documented, of this is by Nadia Abu el-Haj 2001; see also Shavit 1997). Even where the funding of excavation is not motivated directly by a desire for a newsworthy vindication of biblical history, such outcomes are welcomed and publicity is rarely avoided. All too frequently sensational claims are announced well ahead of any sober evaluation, careful analysis, or detailed argumentation. The biblical archaeologist works under many pressures that the historian must recognize, but then discount.

The heyday of biblical archaeology is inseparably connected to the outstanding figure of W. F. Albright, and his massive influence is still being exerted (for an account of Albright and his legacy, see Long 1997). His greatest contribution was his refinement of a system invented by Flinders Petrie of establishing chronology by means of pottery typology. More will be said about this presently. But his influence spread well beyond technique. Albright's belief in the maximal historicity of the Bible gave considerable support to this dogma. Equally important was his adoption of an evolutionary cultural scheme. His *From the Stone Age to Christianity* (1940) and *Archaeology and the Religion of Israel* (1942) sought to trace a single cultural stream through the Bible to modern America, via Christianity. This scheme was made credible by accepting rather uncritically the Bible's own view of its early monotheistic beliefs and of the degeneration of Canaanite culture.

Albright had a conviction that the Bible was historically very reliable. He may to some extent have come to this belief through his archaeology, but undoubtedly he was strongly predisposed to that belief, and his interpretation of the evidence was often biased in its direction. As with an earlier period of biblical archaeology, Albright was in dispute with the conclusions of historical-critical analysis that doubted the historicity of much of the narrative of Genesis–Joshua. He and his followers focused increasingly on two episodes in the Pentateuch that many biblical critics had been questioning: the patriarchal stories and the military conquest of Canaan. The patriarchal stories—especially the life and deeds of Abraham—were not verifiable by excavation, but much use was made of Mesopotamian legal texts recovered in excavation, in which elements of the lifestyle and customs of the patriarchs were held to be reflected. There was a problem in that these texts emanated from different periods, so that a "patriarchal age" could not be very precisely determined, and Albright changed his dating of this period during his career.

The conquest was a different matter: there was evidence of the destruction of Canaanite cities in the Late Bronze Age, and while this did not point exactly to a single complete wave of conquest, there was enough to satisfy Albright that it had occurred. The debate—on both sides—nicely illustrates the near-invisibility of the line between fact and interpretation. A concrete example of Albright's interpretation in this regard is the ancient city of Ai, which had long been identified with the site of et-Tell (both names mean "ruin"). The excavation of the site established clearly that it was not occupied at the time in which the Israelites would have attacked it (Josh. 8). Albright suggested that ancient tradition had moved a story of the conquest of Bethel (Beitin) to Ai. Whether or not Ai is in fact the correct location, there was no archaeological basis for such a suggestion. Had archaeology fitted the biblical evidence, Albright would not have doubted it. The alternative interpretation, advanced by Martin Noth (1971)—that the prominent ruin prompted a legend about its destruction—was rejected, though both explanations presupposed an inaccurate biblical tradition. However, an accidental mistake was preferable to Albright than a deliberate one.

Albright was the son of a Methodist missionary and a biblical literalist. But he was not a fundamentalist. He did not, for instance, accept the historicity of the stories in the early part of Genesis. They were not "scientific." It is unclear whether he had a strict religious commitment to the historical value of the Bible rather than a cultural one. Those who believe in the historicity of the Bible are often accused of religious bias, but many such people are not in fact religious believers. There exists in Western civilization a cultural affection for the Bible and its stories, which I explore in later chapters. Even when a biblical story is viewed as a legend, such as the flood or the destruction of Sodom, there remains a fascination and, it seems, an attraction to the notion that there may be something in it after all.

Despite his aversion to theology, Albright's biblical archaeology nevertheless did bring to birth a distinctive theological position: the biblical theology movement, developed by G. Ernest Wright. In this doctrine, the value of the Bible lay not in its character as Word of God, but in its witness to events. It was in history and not through texts that, in Wright's view, God communicated to humans. Such a view, of course, placed the religious value of the Bible as a hostage to archaeology, and as soon as archaeology began to challenge that witness, such a view could not survive.

In Germany, archaeology was being harnessed in another way by Albrecht Alt and Martin Noth, as a means of critiquing the biblical narrative. For Alt, the occupation of Canaan by Israel was a process of infiltration and sedentarization of seminomads, with military conquest as only a secondary and partial phase. Correspondingly, instead of Wright's biblical theology, and in line with the goals and practices of literary-historical criticism, Noth studied the history of traditions as a way of understanding how the stories grew from events and memories. These considerations will occupy us more fully in a later chapter, but it is only fair to point out that Noth was no Wellhausen, but regarded the pentateuchal tradition as a whole as having been formed at an early stage (before the monarchy). In a less explicit manner than his contemporary von Rad (who was relatively uninterested in archaeology), Noth also stressed Israel's religious distinctiveness among the other nations of antiquity. In retrospect, if Noth was more attentive to a few tensions between archaeology and biblical tradition, the differences between his approach and those of Albright and his followers were not huge.

As a result of recent archaeological work, biblical archaeology is now dead among professional archaeologists. It lives on in the pages of *Biblical Archaeology Review* and in the fundamentalist community that insists archaeology can only ever prove the Bible right and never disprove it. But a highly positive view of archaeology is unfortunately still reflected among the general public, who still retain the notion of archaeology as a science dealing with data and facts and believe that it broadly confirms the Bible as a historical record.

How did it die out? The enterprise as a whole was finally—perhaps belatedly—attacked from within in 1985 by one of Wright's own students, William Dever, who in a number of essays (e.g., Dever 1985) argued that "biblical archaeology" should be redesignated "Syro-Palestinian archaeology" and operate independently of the Bible. The attack was welcomed by many professional archaeologists, but did not result immediately in any discernible change in theory or practice (and Dever has himself reverted entirely to the rhetoric and agenda of "biblical archaeology" [2001]). But the major pillars of the Albright reconstruction, patriarchs and conquest, were already crumbling from a series of attacks by biblical critics, and by the 1970s were being dismantled by new archaeological data.

Doubts about the historicity of an Israelite conquest of Palestine had, as we have just seen, been formulated as early as the 1920s by Albrecht Alt, and his successor Martin Noth developed his ideas both in his own *History of Israel* and his work on the origin of the pentateuchal traditions. There had been a lively transatlantic debate between the advocates of this approach and the Albright school in the mid-twentieth century, which also differed on the existence of a "patriarchal age." But in the 1970s the debate became a North American matter. Thomas Thompson (1974) and John Van Seters (1975) undermined the arguments for a historical patriarchal age. Both showed the archaeology and its derived chronology to be flawed and criticized the notion of a reliable oral tradition, preserving such stories in accurate detail. As for the conquest, another North American scholar, George Mendenhall (1973) suggested that the first Israelites had been Canaanites who revolted against the feudal system and set up, in the highlands, their own egalitarian society. This thesis was elaborated by Norman Gottwald (1979).

Significantly, none of the above scholars was a professional archaeologist. Indeed, their challenges were resisted by many archaeologists and debate might have continued to rage, but for one of the more ironic outcomes of the Six Day War. In 1967 Israel captured and occupied the West Bank, which had been the homeland of Israel and Judah in the first millennium BCE. Access to this region enabled Israeli archaeologists to conduct a survey, later to be elaborated by excavations, of the settlement patterns at the time when ancient Israel had first appeared. The results, which were synthesized by Israel Finkelstein (1988), revealed a group of farming villages in highland clearances, with a material culture that was local. The settlements began in the thirteenth century BCE in the northern (Ephraimite) highlands and, according to Finkelstein's interpretation, appeared in the Judean hills at a later stage. No military conquest seems to have been initially involved in this settlement. These findings challenged the story of a nation arriving from Egypt and taking over the land by force, confronting not just the Albright model but the entire Israeli archaeological tradition, as exemplified by Yigael Yadin, whose excavation at Hazor (1958–64) had sought—and claimed—to find evidence of Joshua's conquest.

Postbiblical Archaeology?

The impact of these results has been felt keenly in North America and Israel, less so in Europe where, as we have seen, the outcome was to some extent anticipated. Albright's views and the biblical theology movement have been largely abandoned, while Israeli archaeology, which had been closely linked to the Zionist project of reclaiming Palestine for Jews, moved into a post-Zionist phase. In both countries dismay and resistance to this new landscape are still in evidence, and a number of discoveries, both genuine and counterfeit, have served to refresh arguments for biblical historicity. But in large measure the debate has shifted from the premonarchic era to the time of David and Solomon, for the existence of a united monarchy based in Jerusalem is also under threat from archaeological reasoning (see below). In short, while archaeology has made some definitive contributions to the understanding of Israelite and Judean origins, a good deal of controversy remains, which is ideologically highly charged.

With the publication of the West Bank Survey, archaeologists ceased to resist those biblical scholars who were focusing on the Pentateuch as a *tradition* whose historicity was problematic, and instead began to provide a basis for a history of Israelite settlement—and Israelite origins—that was different from the biblical story and independent of it. The role of the biblical narrative as a kind of basic draft of history, to be confirmed or qualified by archaeology, is no longer possible without relegating archaeology to a secondary and rather intermittent role, and indeed abusing it in the process, because archaeological data cannot deliver a history similar to the biblical story. The capacity of archaeology to provide a truly independent account of Palestine's past is now being envisaged, and two books have already been published which attempt just that, by Israel Finkelstein and Neil Asher Silberman (2001, 2006). Nevertheless, these cannot be regarded as fully independent accounts: biblical data, for example, on the reign of Josiah, still furnish a major basis of the history. But priority is given to the archaeological evidence, and the method of integrating the two sets of data is a considerable advance on previous ones. It remains questionable how far a purely archaeological history can go beyond describing the everyday life of ancient Palestinians. Integrating the biblical narratives into this archaeological horizon is certainly a necessary task, but one with limited possibilities (see further in chap. 6).

One of the major issues of postbiblical archaeology that still has to be addressed is the definition of the biblical period. This term has long been taken to mean the period with which the Bible deals (from almost any point in the past to the end of the fifth century), and this was previously regarded also as the time when the major biblical texts were created. Biblical archaeology therefore focused on the Middle and Late Bronze ages (c. 2200–1250 BCE) and the Iron Age. In recent years there has been a much greater interest in the neo-Babylonian and Persian periods as the context for much of the biblical literature. Unfortunately, however, the degree of attention paid to these periods has been much less, and the results are less extensive and less reliable. It must also be admitted, however, that extrabiblical literary sources for this period are also less than for the ninth–seventh centuries.

Using archaeology rather than the biblical story as the basis is methodologically sounder, because we have a better control over the interpretation of the data. But this control is still partial and the results subject to disagreement. That the archaeology itself is carefully interrogated is vital, yet it can be difficult: archaeologists have not always offered the detailed evidence on which their con-clusions are based until some time after these conclusions have been delivered; indeed, this is often impossible. Only with the full excavation report can the data and the reasoning be thoroughly checked. Obviously excavators are under pressure to announce findings in good time, but such preliminary reports should be regarded as provisional. Furthermore, interpretation often involves a comparison of different sites, especially where chronology is at stake, and correlations are only possible when the data from all the sites are carefully interpreted: even then, one must allow for mar-gins of error. At the present time, for example, there is a dis-agreement between archaeologists on the basic chronology of the period of the so-called united monarchy and on the occupation of Jerusalem in the tenth–ninth centuries.

Archaeological Practice

In the second part of this chapter we should therefore turn from archaeological agendas and issues and look briefly at a few aspects of archaeological practice of which historians and their readers need to be aware. In general, at the beginnings of Middle (Near) Eastern archaeology, the major goals of archaeology were to uncover structures and recover artifacts, for display as well as for scientific reasons—and these goals are still pursued, of course. But increasingly the aim has been to discover everything possible about the site and its inhabitants—including, for example, its ecology, its place within the region, its trade patterns, and its population size and distribution. The aim of a modern archaeological campaign is to preserve as accurately as possible a record of everything that is excavated. After all, excavation destroys much of the evidence, and the damage is justified only by replacing the previous state of the physical remains by a fully recorded and organized record of not only what was found, but exactly where.

Urban Excavation

The archaeology of Palestine has never been systematic. It has already been explained that a focus on what was regarded as the biblical period (the Iron Age) and on sites that might be mentioned in the Bible has created an imbalance in our knowledge. Because biblical archaeology was more concerned to illuminate the Bible than the past (though on the assumption that there was not much difference), the targets for excavation were the large mounds that betrayed the presence of cities that might be identified with places mentioned in the Bible—such as Megiddo, Jericho, Hazor, Lachish, and Gezer. The identifications of these places with the biblical names are largely resolved, though some doubts remain. Bethel is one of these, although a majority view identifies it with Beitin. Next to Jerusalem it is the most frequently mentioned cultic site in Palestine, but its sanctuary has not yet been discovered. As a result, we cannot actually write the archaeological history of Bethel, but only of the site with which we identify it. In any case, neither of the two most likely sites has been adequately excavated; the dig at Beitin was badly conducted and overinterpreted from biblical data. El-Bireh, the other candidate, has not been excavated at all (and hence remains a hypothetical alternative). Hence, if the historian wishes to know whether Bethel was really sacked by Josiah, or if it was abandoned when Samaria was converted into an Assyrian province, or if it remained in use during the neo-Babylonian period, we cannot fully rely on archaeology to answer these questions, for a number of reasons.

Ancient cities take the form of large mounds (*tells* or *tels*) created by the accumulation of successive periods of occupation; each later layer is typically built on the ruins of the previous one. But this process does not necessarily happen at once or uniformly; different buildings or city quarters can be rebuilt at any time. Only with major rebuilding or destruction do we find a major break. Hence, excavation exploits both horizontal and vertical dimensions. According to the usual practice, the site to be excavated is divided into squares so that everything found can be spatially registered, while the baulks (walls) that emerge between the squares as they are excavated reveal the vertical layers (strata) of occupation. The horizontal mapping of the site allows a reconstruction of the shape of the site at a particular period, while the vertical reveals the chronological sequence of very precise points that can subsequently be correlated. Both operations are in fact conducted at the same time and as part of the same excavation procedure.

The basis of archaeological chronology is therefore stratigraphy (which in turn permits pottery typology; see below). But it is not necessarily the case that everything in a lower stratum is earlier than what is in a higher one: foundation trenches, erosion, pits, debris falling through gaps, or the work of burrowing animals can all disturb the sequence. The remains of buildings usually extend upward through many strata since structures can be rebuilt or reused. Finding the floor levels of each structure is crucial, and dating them depends on identifying the pottery associated with each one. Whatever is found immediately under the floor gives the earliest date at which the building could have been constructed, while pottery on the floor of the building gives the latest date at which it may have been constructed. But it must not be forgotten that the most common building material is not stone but mud brick. Floors and buildings are often represented by no more than compressed earth, unlike monumental architecture in stone.

Stratigraphy provides only a relative sequence, not an absolute chronology. The analysis of pottery forms (ceramic typology) enables the strata in which they are found to be put into a wider context and given a little more chronological precision. Pottery types each have their own life cycle. Some persist over a long time;

others are of shorter duration. Some kinds of vessels remain in use longer (e.g., luxury items, storage jars); others (cooking and eating vessels) are replaced more frequently. But pottery forms all go in and out of fashion, though often over long periods. An assemblage of pottery forms associated with a particular stratum can therefore provide an indication of relative date because the period at which all the forms can have existed simultaneously is shorter than the life of any one pottery form. This kind of analysis of pottery is called seriation, and the history of excavation has produced a well-established typology of forms that corresponds to a chronological sequence.

The seriation of pottery from a particular stratum at one site can thus enable the stratum to be correlated chronologically with other strata at other sites. If a destruction layer or a building foundation at one site can be connected with a recorded event, however, the dating of the event can be transferred to the corresponding strata at other sites.

This (simplified) account of how pottery is used for dating may give the impression that it is highly scientific. But a great deal still depends on interpretation, and no conclusions about dating should be taken as scientifically proven. All pottery and stratigraphic chronology is, in the end, relative, and the most famous "absolute" dates, such as the destruction of Late Bronze Age Hazor and the Solomonic cities, have since been abandoned. Like history, archaeology is the art of reading a narrative from data, but archaeology does at least work with hard data and employs scientific techniques.

Indeed, science can offer other techniques for absolute dating, though so far only within a certain range that increases as we go further back. In the case of Iron Age Palestine, carbon-14 dating can be usefully applied (see Levy and Higham 2005). This is a completely scientific measurement of YBP (Years Before Present) based on measurement of a carbon isotope with consistent rate of decay from the moment it ceases to be organic. But it is necessary to realize that different tests (and different laboratories) can and do yield different results. This variation has less to do with the actual materials than with differences in the manner and conduct of tests. Some divergence is at present inevitable, and complete agreement would have to be viewed with suspicion. Yet even if the results closely agree they will always express the conclusions in terms of probability, and here some further misunderstanding is possible.

To take a hypothetical example: there might be a 40 percent probability that the date arrived at lies between 2500 and 2400 YBP (= 491–391 BCE). The probability increases toward 100 percent as the span is lengthened, but over a shorter period it decreases. The more precise the figure needed, the less the probability. Moreover, within any given range, the probability is equal. The year 441 BCE would be no more likely than either 491 or 391. Averaging out different test results is also unreliable. So, as we shall see below, radiocarbon data do not (at present) resolve dating questions that require a fairly close margin and a long time in the past.

Other scientific dating methods, such as fluorine or nitrogen analysis of bones, provide only relative dates among samples from a similar location. Dendrochronology, which provides data on the age of living trees by counting rings that represent years of growth, can, however, be integrated with carbon-14 dates to provide a more accurate correlation. But such calculations (as far as I know) have not yet been produced for ancient Palestine. As we shall see in the next chapter, for the present it is only literary sources that provide absolute chronology for historical periods, and while these are very good from about the eighth century, there can be no certainty before this.

Excavation results are always partial. Tells are never excavated entirely, for good reasons: not just economic, but also in order to leave scope for future digs with better resources. But they are not always excavated equally, either. If the period in which the archaeologist is interested happens to be the biblical period (defined as the Iron Age or earlier, ca. 1250–500), then strata belonging to the *later* periods will of course be encountered first if the site has been occupied later (as is usual). This material is in the way in two senses: it is physically overlying earlier strata and has to be dug through, but it also presents an obstacle when the main focus of the dig lies elsewhere. It takes time and effort to deal correctly with such data, and that in turn delays (and adds to the costs). The evidence from later layers is not necessarily ignored or disregarded; but it is fair to say that the relative neglect of such data in the past means that while our archaeological knowledge of the Iron Age occupation of Palestine is rather good, it is much less good for later periods.

Tell archaeology is a complex operation and its interpretation even more so. It does not produce raw historical data in the sense of implying a narrative. Even less does it confirm a historical event. It can indicate processes, but assigning these to specific historical moments is a matter of compatibility with data from elsewhere. Thus, to take a famous example, the discovery of monumental triple gateways and casemate walls at Hazor, Megiddo, and Gezer does not prove that these cities were (re)built by Solomon, who is described in 1 Kings as having done so. Indeed, it is now generally agreed that these features do not belong exclusively to the time assigned to Solomon nor are they unique to Palestine. Their existence might furnish an explanation of why they are mentioned in the Bible and why they may have been thought to have been built by a great king. It might be reasonable to conclude that the rebuilding of the cities was correctly remembered but not the builder. Indeed, archaeology cannot tell us, either, that these gates and walls were the product of a single builder. Independent city-states might well rebuild according to the most advanced techniques of fortification and, if all destroyed in a single military campaign from an invader, they would build simultaneously.

The most valuable artifacts for purposes of dating are inscribed objects, as long as their exact provenance can be established. Objects acquired from dealers, whether legitimately or not, are of little use when it cannot be confirmed where they were found. Even the two fragments of the recently celebrated "Tel Dan stela" were both found in secondary contexts; that is, they had been reused in antiquity for another purpose. The Siloam inscription is a different case: nearly everyone assumes it was inscribed (along with the tunnel) during Hezekiah's reign. But unusually, no royal name at all is given—not on the inscription, nor any data that would tell us who built it and when. In recent years, some inscriptions have also surfaced that turned out to be forgeries. But these will all be discussed in the next chapter.

Example: The Problem of the United Monarchy

To end the section on excavation, we can look in more detail at a crucial period in biblical and archaeological history about which there is a serious disagreement: the period during which David or Solomon would have ruled over a united Israel and Judah. The beginning of Iron I in Palestine (c. 1250 BCE) is marked by a clear cultural break: the urban-agricultural system of Late Bronze—already in decline—gives way to a more pastoral agricultural system based on villages—though not entirely: some cities continued in existence alongside the new villages. According to the conventional chronology of this era (now known as the "high chronology"), another major factor is the arrival of the Philistines; in 1175, the Pharaoh Rameses II, having repulsed the Sea Peoples from the Nile delta, allowed or encouraged them to settle on the Palestinian coastal plain. Their presence is marked by a distinctive pottery, locally made but of foreign design, and monochrome. After a few decades this gives way to bichrome pottery, which lasts until about 1000 when Philistine power wanes. It is tempting to correlate this Philistine decline with the reign of David; in any event it marks the transition from Iron IB to Iron IIA, which is signalled by the six-chambered gates at Hazor, Megiddo, and Gezer and by the appearance of red-slip and burnished pottery.

In 1996 Israel Finkelstein proposed a revision of this chronology. He argued that excavated artifacts demonstrate continuing Egyptian rule in Palestine beyond 1175 with no evidence of mixed Philistine and Egyptian material culture at the major military centers such as Lachish, Megiddo, and Bethshean. At Tel Miqne (Ekron) and Ashdod, two major Philistine cities, monochrome ware is separated from Egyptian ware, and found in later strata. Hence, the Philistines did not settle until the 1140s or 1130s, after Egyptian withdrawal. The appearance of their distinctive bichrome ware must therefore be assigned to 1100 and lasts until almost 900, when the beginning of Iron II should be dated.

As for the supposed Solomonic architecture at Hazor, Megiddo, and Gezer, Finkelstein argues that its dating has been derived only from the biblical reference in 1 Kings 9:15, and that this correlation has been extrapolated to other sites. But other data bring this biblical portrait into doubt: Jerusalem was at the time a small unfortified village; Judah itself had a very small population and no monumental architecture—in short, no signs of the infrastructure necessary for a state of any significance. The Davidic-Solomonic empire cannot, as a consequence, be the explanation for the monumental architecture in major cities of Israel.

The "low chronology" proposed by Finkelstein dates the Solomonic architecture and its associated pottery to Omri (886–874), whom the Assyrians (and others) regarded as the founder of Israel. As a consequence, everything dated on the high chronology to the tenth century (the supposed time of David and Solomon) is now to be redated to the ninth, leaving the tenth century as a rather large gap.

Finkelstein's major opponent is Amihai Mazar (1997), who has nevertheless proposed, mainly in the light of results from his own excavations in Tel Rehov, a modification of the high chronology (and thus a compromise) that has reduced the difference from about a century to fifty years (Bruins, van der Plicht, Mazar 2003). The debate continues, each side claiming victory and also appealing to radiocarbon dates. A great deal, of course, hangs on the outcome.

This dispute extends also to the interpretation of a building uncovered with great publicity by Eilat Mazar in the City of David, the Ophel hill, site of Iron Age Jerusalem. Mazar calls the building a "Large Stone Structure" and dates it to about 1000 BCE, identifying it as the palace of King David. (A. Mazar supports her.) Eilat Mazar's interpretation has, not surprisingly, been challenged (Finkelstein, Herzog, Singer-Avitz, and Ussishkin 2007). Their conclusion is that the structure consists of several elements, all of which postdate the Iron I/Iron IIA transition (which in any case they date later than Mazar), and most seem to belong to the late Hellenistic period. The point to be made here is not about the rightness of either side, but about the huge uncertainty that archaeological interpretation can involve—in this case, over a millennium for some parts of the structure.

In the light of such disagreement among well-qualified archaeologists, what can the historian do? What sort of early Israel is the historian to write about? It may be worth reminding ourselves that ancient history, and especially that of Judah and Israel, has a modern dimension. Perhaps the ancient world seems different in secular Tel Aviv than in religious (not to mention Davidic) Jerusalem?

Survey, Demography, Ecology

If architecture makes a more dramatic impact on the public imagination and artifacts on museum (and private) collections, other forms of archaeological research have provided the modern historian with equally important data in recent years. History is not necessarily a story of states or cities, where physical records are more detailed and concentrated; it is also a story of social change, population shifts and growth, and exploitation of natural resources. The majority of ancient inhabitants of Palestine did not live in cities, but in the countryside. Cities (in most cases, "town" is a better term, given the size) had their own hinterland, of course, which included rural areas that provided most of the wealth as well as the subsistence. Most villages belonged to a town or city (see Josh. 21:10–15 for an instance), especially in the sense that their produce was subject to taxation from its ruler. But the earliest Iron Age inhabitants of the Palestinian highlands did not necessarily depend on cities—though in some cases this may well have happened, for several Late Bronze Age towns, such as Mazar's Tel Rehov, or Megiddo, continued into the Iron Age.

Surveys can provide information about the human use of the landscape in general—settlement, agriculture, trade routes, fortification, and defense, even seasonal migration. They are indispensable in regional studies. Rather than merely as a preparation for excavation, surveys are now used in their own right as sources of data. They can be systematic or not, extensive or intensive, depending on the area being surveyed and the resources available to survey it.

Like excavation, the results of surveys need to be read with some caution. Among the factors affecting the reliability of a survey can be the number of surveyors employed for the area being surveyed, visibility, time of year, weather, and vegetation. When pottery or other remains from a specific period are being sought, material from later occupation can also obscure it. The gathering and interpreting of data from various surveys can also depend on the quantity of identifiable pottery and differences in interpretation between surveyors. Extrapolating from the results is also a matter of judgment, and estimates of population from the findings are far from certain. Obviously the wider and more thorough the survey, the better the data. In the case of the West Bank survey, figures from the Ottoman period were used as an aid in calculating population densities in the Iron Age. But the calculations are nevertheless hypothetical; the size of households and the extent of the site over time can both vary, as can crop yields.

Fluctuations in population densities, indicated by settlement numbers and size, can betray climatic, economic, and political changes. The exploitation of people and resources was one of the mechanisms of imperial Assyrian administration followed by its successors. The Assyrians practiced transportation to populate areas that were short of human resources as well as in order to punish rebellious vassal states and pacify territories. Empires require large income, which needed to be achieved not merely through tribute (which depends on economic capacity) but through increasing trade (and so taxes on it) and greater agricultural efficiency. Tributary kingdoms were of course obliged to maximize agricultural revenue, and crops that could be traded for silver or, later, coinage. Imperial rulers could also undertake such initiatives. Hence, for example, olive oil production in southern Palestine in the seventh century was industrialized, with a processing facility at Ekron (Tel Miqne).

The interpretation of population movement can be controversial, however. What follows are some examples of survey data and their "conversion" into history.

Judah and Jerusalem in the Eighth–Seventh Centuries

In the last quarter of the eighth century BCE, Samaria was captured and the kingdom of Israel dismantled, replaced by three Assyrian provinces. At around this time, the city of Jerusalem grew enormously. But Judah was also invaded by the Assyrian king Sennacherib and widely devastated. The growth of the city can be shown through urban excavation—but to explain the growth, and indeed to explain the chain of cause and effect, it is necessary to find from where the population came. One theory is that the newcomers were refugees from Israel, recently destroyed by Assyria and converted into three provinces. Surveys seem to show that the growth in Judah was accompanied by a decrease in the southern part of the former kingdom of Israel belonging to Ephraim and Benjamin, supporting the theory of an influx into Judah. Another theory is that they fled from the devastated Judean countryside because of the Assyrian depradations. But is it natural that farmers would leave their lands or that they would be driven out? If so, they would hardly flee to a city, except for temporary refuge. On either explanation, long-term urban expansion is not the likely outcome. Such growth implies an upturn in economic activity that would support an increase in nonagricultural population (such as merchants, artisans, administrators).

Another problem is that these explanations suppose that the growth of the city occurred under Hezekiah—and perhaps the biblical portrait of this king has influenced some of the interpretation. But what if the growth took place largely under Hezekiah's successor, Manasseh? Archaeology cannot determine the date with sufficient precision to rule out the seventh century. Both interpretations, of course, fit with the biblical story, according to which Hezekiah, a good king, saw his country devastated and had to pay a large tribute, while Manasseh, a bad king, apparently pleased the Assyrians and so may have reigned over a peaceful and prosperous Judah.

The Neo-Babylonian and Persian Period: *Jerusalem to Mizpah and Back*

Surveys also contribute greatly to our understanding of the life of Judah between the fall of Jerusalem in 586 and the advent of Cyrus. The biblical story takes little interest in this period, since its Israel is in exile and the land is (theologically) empty. We get only an account of the first few years, then silence. But surveys might be able to tell us more of what happened, at least in the fifth century, when some repopulation in Judah can be detected.

When the kingdom of Judah ended—or, more precisely, when Jerusalem was destroyed and its ruling dynasty removed—the . kingdom, either still as a kingdom or as a province, was administered from Mizpah (about 10 kilometers/6.5 miles to the north of Jerusalem). The actual boundaries of the kingdom/province are still disputed, but there was undoubtedly a shift in the center of gravity. Much of the population in and around Jerusalem was deported, and much of it fled, since the Babylonian assault had been concentrated on Jerusalem. It is estimated (from surveys) that the population in and around Jerusalem fell by 90 percent and may have been initially zero. In the south, different populations (Edomite, Arabian) immigrated. The major areas of settlement in Judah were around Bethlehem and in the territory of Benjamin. The Beersheba valley was also nearly deserted. But from the end of the sixth century, the Benjaminite population began to decline (for a detailed discussion and interpretation, see Lipschits 2005). Here again, we should nevertheless beware of the influence of biblical information. The date of the population shift to Benjamin is indicated not only by the biblical narrative but by the Babylonian Chronicle and its confirmation of the fall of the city and deportation of many inhabitants. That seems a reliable date. But we have no inscriptional evidence relating to the restoration of Jerusalem, and the biblical evidence is rather uncertain (Neh. 1:3, apparently set in the mid-fifth century, still speaks of Jerusalem as a ruined city). The process by which Jerusalem resumed its former role certainly took place, and there was repopulation from Babylonia. But was this sudden, or gradual, and when did it occur? The survey data permit some partial answers only (for a detailed analysis and synthesis, see Edelman 2005).

Charting the "return" to Jerusalem is quite difficult, even with survey data. The fact is that not many Persian period levels in Judah have been excavated. Moreover, distinguishing between pottery of the late monarchic (Iron IIC), neo-Babylonian, and Persian eras is not easy, nor is it possible to date pottery within the Persian period (538–332). It is also important to distinguish sites occupied in the neo-Babylonian *and* Persian periods from those settled only in the Persian period. The figures given in the detailed analysis of Edelman (2005) are: sites with Iron II pottery but no Persian, 372; with both, 154. The former were probably abandoned in or just before 586, and 108 were newly settled under the Persians. Of these 48 were sites formerly occupied (Iron IIB/C); 60 were therefore on virgin land. They cluster in five areas: Benjamin, the central Judean hill country, the Shephelah (the foothills), southeast of Lachish, and the southern Judean highlands (Edelman 2005; see her map on 57).

A set of administrative settlements has also been traced from survey; these form a roughly north-south and east-west line; the north-south follows the long-established trade route; the east-west does not. But they cross at Jerusalem. Were these still marking trade routes, or defensive lines? Or were they relay stations for fire signals? Each settlement has a cluster of farmsteads in the vicinity. The picture suggests some kind of policy (presumably imperial) rather than a random settlement by individual immigrants. The interpretation of all this is of course uncertain, but the historian will have to rely on these results in deciding why, when, and how Judah was resettled under the Persians. The biblical accounts can then be interpreted accordingly. But they give no explanation of when and why Jerusalem took over again from Mizpah. On the state of relations between Jerusalem and Samaria, however, neither the biblical narrative nor the survey data are of much help. The Jewish papyri from Elephantine in Egypt suggest that Samaria and Jerusalem were both seen as having some responsibility for the colony's temple; Nehemiah's suggestion of

Samaritan opposition may reflect later antagonism. Archaeology is unlikely to be able to help.

Ethnicity

Finally, we should consider ethnicity. Can archaeology—in which ethnicity has been a key topic in recent years—help to determine who was an Israelite, who a Judean, and who not? The answer is that it depends on what is meant by "ethnicity." As currently defined (see Jones 1997, Miller 2008) it is not merely a matter of genetic makeup. This may seem at first sight to be the biblical definition, but genealogies seem to function as reflections of ethnic affiliation and not as causes: they are compiled and adjusted to reflect perceptions of social relations. But nor is ethnicity merely a matter of material culture. Whether archaeology can reveal ethnicity is particularly relevant to ancient Palestine, at least where the historian is concerned with Israel and Judah. If it is the case, for example, that (as even the biblical stories admit) the population of the kingdom of Israel contained many different racial elements, then an "Israelite" might be a Phoenician or a Hittite or a Philistine or Moabite or Aramean by birth or ancestry. There are problems with many of the marks of ethnicity attributed to Israelites or, later, to Jews. Circumcision, for example, was practiced by most Semites and Egyptians (possibly even some Philistines), and cannot have functioned as an exclusive mark of Jewish identity until perhaps the Greco-Roman era when it became something of a curiosity. In any case, Genesis makes it a mark of all Abrahamic nations, perhaps most of the inhabitants of the Persian satrapy of Across the River, between the Euphrates and the Mediterranean. Avoidance of pork is also not necessarily unique to Israelites or Judeans and may originally have more to do with ecology: pigs do not provide milk or cheese and may thus be unsuitable for certain lifestyles. What makes an Israelite archaeologically recognizable? Culturally, there is nothing that can tell an archaeologist whether something is Israelite or not, except by inference from its location in an Israelite city. Judaism, however, is culturally distinct, and can be recognized by the occasional use of the Hebrew language, by tefillin (phylacteries), mezuzot, ritual baths, and other indications. However, most archaeologists now accept that Israel did not originate as a distinct ethnic group but *became* one. The Israel addressed by archaeology does not have the same origins, history, religion, or culture as the biblical Israel. Indeed, there is no archaeological evidence that the populations of Israel and Judah even formed a single people or nation; there is no archaeological basis for calling Judah "Israel." So, in what sense are the Iron Age highland farmers to be called "proto-Israelites"? In the sense that they will later form a kingdom of Israel? But that kingdom also included urban populations with a different history. The fundamental issue in relating archaeology and the Bible is that they do not speak about the same Israel. This is perhaps the most serious dilemma for the modern historian. How do we get from one to the other? How do we relate them?

Summary

Archaeology provides a basis for a material history of the inhabitants of ancient Palestine, but its evidence is partial because of the nature of the data and the selectivity of excavation and surveys. A good deal of previous archaeological research is also suspect because the interpretation has sometimes been based on biblical data; indeed, most archaeological work until the 1970s was concerned with defending or illuminating the biblical accounts of the past rather than offering independent assessment.

In any case, the interpretation of archaeological data is often controversial; even apart from the ongoing agenda of verifying the Bible—which is still present in some archaeology—there can be legitimate difference of opinion on crucial matters. None of this means that the relevance of archaeology should be minimized, but reasonable scope must be left for revision of findings. In particular, provisional or premature claims based on recent work should always be taken carefully, especially where the excavation is sponsored by organizations whose agenda is not purely scholarly.

References

Abu el-Haj, Nadia
2001   *Facts on the Ground: Archaeological Practice and Territorial Self-Fashioning in Israeli Society*, Chicago: University of Chicago Press.

Albright, William F.
1940   *From the Stone Age to Christianity*, Baltimore: Johns Hopkins Press (2nd ed., 1946, 1957)

1942   *Archaeology and the Religion of Israel*, Baltimore: Johns Hopkins Press.

Bruins, Hendrik J., Johannes van der Plicht, and Amihai Mazar
2003   "14C Dates from Tel Rehov: Iron-Age Chronology, Pharaohs, and Hebrew Kings," *Science* 300:315–18.

Davis, Thomas W.
2004   *Shifting Sands: The Rise and Fall of Biblical Archaeology*, Oxford: Oxford University Press.

Dever, William
1985   "Syro-Palestinian and Biblical Archaeology," in D. A. Knight and G. M. Tucker (eds.), *The Hebrew Bible and Its Modern Interpreters*, Chico, Calif.: Scholars Press, 31–74.

2001   *What Did the Biblical Writers Know and When Did They Know It? What Archaeology Can Tell Us about the Reality of Ancient Israel*, Grand Rapids: Eerdmans.

Edelman, Diana
2005   *The Origins of the "Second Temple": Persian Imperial Policy and the Rebuilding of Jerusalem*, London: Equinox.

Finkelstein, Israel
1988   *The Archaeology of the Israelite Settlement*, Jerusalem: Israel Exploration Society.

1996   "The Archaeology of the United Monarchy: An Alternative View," *Levant* 28:177–87.

Finkelstein, Israel, and Neil Asher Silberman
2001   *The Bible Unearthed: Archaeology's New Vision of Ancient Israel and the Origin of Its Sacred Texts*, New York: Free Press.

2006   *David and Solomon: In Search of the Bible's Sacred Kings and the Roots of the Western Tradition*, New York: Free Press.

Finkelstein, Israel, Ze'ev Herzog, Lily Singer-Avitz, and David Ussishkin
2007   "Has King David's Palace in Jerusalem Been Found?" *Tel Aviv* 34:142–64.

Gottwald, Norman K.
1979   *The Tribes of Yahweh: A Sociology of the Religion of Liberated Israel*, Maryknoll, N.Y.: Orbis, 1979; Sheffield: Sheffield Academic Press, 1999.

Herzog, Z.
    2007   Cited in "Digging Biblical History at the End of the World," in *Science Daily*, November 21.

Jones, Sian
    1997   *The Archaeology of Ethnicity: Constructing Identities in the Past and Present*, London and New York: Routledge.

Levy, Thomas E., and Thomas Higham
    2005   *The Bible and Radiocarbon Dating*, London: Equinox.

Lipschits, Oded
    2005   *The Fall and Rise of Jerusalem*, Winona Lake, Ind.: Eisenbrauns.

Long, Burke O.
    1997   *Planting and Reaping Albright: Politics, Ideology, and Interpreting the Bible*, University Park: Pennsylvania State University Press.

Mazar, Amihai
    1997   "Iron Age Chronology: A Reply to I. Finkelstein," *Levant* 29:157–67.

Mendenhall, George E.
    1973   *The Tenth Generation: The Origins of the Biblical Tradition*, Baltimore: Johns Hopkins University Press.

Miller, James C.
    1988   "Ethnicity and the Hebrew Bible: Problems and Prospects," *Currents in Biblical Research* 6:170–213.

Noth, Martin
    1971   *Das Buch Josua*, 3rd ed., Tübingen: Mohr.

Shavit, Yaacov
    1997   "Archaeology, Political Culture, and Culture in Israel," in N. A. Silberman and D. B. Small (eds.), *The Archaeology of Israel: Constructing the Past, Interpreting the Present*, Sheffield: Sheffield Academic Press, 48–61.

Silberman, Neil Asher
    1982   *Digging for God and Country: Exploration, Archeology, and the Secret Struggle for the Holy Land, 1799–1917*, New York: Knopf.

Thompson, Thomas L.
    1974   *The Historicity of the Patriarchal Narratives*, Berlin: de Gruyter.

Van Seters, John
    1975   *Abraham in History and Tradition*, New Haven, Conn.: Yale University Press.

Chapter Five

Epigraphic Sources

Inscriptions have traditionally been very important in shedding light on certain episodes in the biblical histories, and have often seemed the most straightforward. Though they are usually retrieved in the course of archaeological excavation, they are not like other material artifacts, which rely totally on the expertise of the interpreter to give them meaning. The discovery of inscriptions containing names of characters mentioned in the Bible was one of the earliest stimuli to the revival of a belief in the historical veracity of the biblical histories, and the existence of such names does at least verify that these stories are not uninformed about real persons and events.

It is useful to distinguish, with Millard (1972), three kinds of inscription: monumental, occasional, and professional. The first is for public display; the second includes graffiti, (unofficial) letters, and seals; the third is the product of official scribes. It would, in fact, be useful to subdivide the last category into documentary works, serving purely pragmatic purposes (receipts, ration lists, all forms of bookkeeping, astronomical observations), and texts where rhetorical and literary considerations need to be given (omen lists, diplomatic correspondence, wisdom texts). The historical value of each kind, at any rate, needs to be assessed differently.

Inscriptions and Chronology

Arguably the most important information we can extract from inscriptions is precise dating. But the most common method of ancient dating was by the regnal years of kings (though in chap. 2 we saw that these might be amenable to manipulation). The Assyrians additionally kept lists giving the name of the highest-ranking official (called the *limmu*) each year, which also sometimes mention an important event during that year. These have been preserved from what we can now date as 911 to 631 BCE. In the second century CE the astronomer Ptolemy integrated lists of kings and regnal years with astronomical data from ancient Babylonia and Assyria and was thus able to produce a sequential calendar from Nabonassar (whom we now date to 747–734) to Cleopatra (51–31 BCE), and his data served as the basis for many subsequent calendars. We can calculate absolute dates from Ptolemy's data (and directly from the *limmu* lists) because certain years witnessed solar eclipses. According to one *limmu* list, a solar eclipse occurred in the tenth regnal year of the Assyrian king Assurdan II, in the month of Sivan (May–June). We can now verify that there was an eclipse in 763 BCE. The *limmu* lists thus give us an exact chronology from there up to 631 BCE, and by working out that the Assyrians captured the Egyptian city of Thebes in 664 BCE, we gain a peg in Egyptian chronology. From the introduction of coinage to the ancient Middle East in the Persian era, we are also able to correlate chronologies in several regions. For the Persian empire onward we can also use the accounts of Greek historians (especially Herodotus, who in fact provides more knowledge of that empire than Persian sources), and other Hellenistic historians such as Berossus (Babylonia), Manetho (Egypt), Philo (Byblos), and, somewhat later, Josephus. These historians are of value, of course, only where they have been able to use earlier (reliable) sources. But given the widespread interest in historiography in the Hellenistic era, the range of sources available to the modern historian is transformed from earlier periods.

But if we want to calculate backward from Nabonassar, we rely mostly on names of monarchs and their regal years. We also need to use Egyptian chronology, which is not absolutely secure. In fact, Egyptian dates have in the past been derived from biblical dates and biblical dates from Egyptian ones, in circular fashion. At present, we should be wary of any absolute dates given for events in Palestine (and most other places) before the seventh century. Indeed, the inscriptional coverage of historical events in Palestine does not go much further back. The Merneptah stele from the late thirteenth century provides some evidence of names and claimed conquests, including a probable reference to Israel. Otherwise, the earliest biblical individual to whom any inscription makes a direct reference is Omri king of Israel, whom we can date (very probably) early in the eighth century, though in most cases it is his dynasty or "house" that is mentioned, and not the king himself.

Documentary Texts

This category consists of texts that are created for pragmatic purposes, and have no deliberate literary or ideological function. They are not what nowadays we would call "literature." But the boundaries between these and "literary texts" are not absolutely clear-cut. Letters, for example, can be treated as documentary as they are intended only to communicate information; literary letters are a well-known genre that attempt much more. The letters written from Lachish during Sennacherib's invasion in 701 give not only a dramatic account but also a more reliable insight than official accounts. They would not fulfill their function if they misled. By contrast, official accounts may be intended to mislead, and would reflect the royal ideology on either side. The letters from the Judean colony in Elephantine from fifth–fourth centuries BCE, being examples of diplomatic correspondence, are, however, more likely to express a viewpoint or even to present the facts in a less than honest light; they are, after all, part of a negotiation process. The ostraca from Kuntillet Ajrud, invoking blessing from "Yhwh and his Asherah" (as most modern interpreters understand it), shed more reliable light on everyday religious practice and belief than texts that might prescribe what *should* be done or believed. The handling of such sources belongs to the basic repertoire of the modern historian of any period, and it is unfortunate that we have so few for ancient Palestine.

It is important to distinguish such documentary texts from literary examples that seem quite similar in genre. The *limmu* lists and the *Neo-Babylonian Chronicles* are documentary; their value (ancient as well as modern) depends on their recording accurately. The *Sumerian King List*, however, which gives the names of rulers "before the Flood," is not a contemporary chronicle and lies closer to mythology, as we may suspect do the prediluvian names in Genesis. But generic markers are not always clear. Ancient genealogies, which appear factual and documentary (like modern family trees), will almost certainly contain a good deal of correct information about lineage. But their social and political (or even religious) function is paramount, and they can at times verge on the purely fictitious when making a claim to a particular ancestry. We need, therefore, to concentrate on other kinds of epigraphic sources.

Monumental Inscriptions

No monumental inscription of a Judean or Israelite king has survived. But since there is (see below) one Aramean and one Moabite inscription, it is likely that they once existed; if so, the reasons for their nonsurvival are unknown.

Assyrian inscriptions relevant to biblical history mostly fall into the monumental category, comprising display inscriptions and annals. Display inscriptions are used, for example, as "wallpaper" inside the palace or in other prominent places on walls or gates. While they refer, more or less, to real events, they are not intended to offer sober and accurate accounts so much as to generate an effect. Their language and content conform to the literary and political (and graphic) conventions of the genre, and they are almost always created for reasons of propaganda, emphasizing the success of the king and the greatness of Assyria and its god. Displays tend to be structured not so much by chronology as by spatiality, or by topic. Differences can therefore be seen between displays of the same event(s), and of course with an annalistic account where that is also available.

Perhaps the best-known example of this kind of inscription is the Lachish frieze in the British Museum, where different stages of the siege are depicted in different places. Baruch Halpern (2001, 107–32) gives a very entertaining account, detailing effects such as altering the sequence of events, pauses in the narrative, repetition, and, of course, exaggeration of royal prowess. Minor victories, and even nonvictories, become major ones. It goes without saying that any indecisive encounter will certainly be claimed as a victory by both sides, as at the battle of Qarqar, where in the ninth century BCE Shalmaneser III of Assyria met a coalition of Syrian and Palestinian forces that included Ahab the Israelite. The Assyrian king's stele gives a highly bombastic account of a great victory. Halpern's contention is that we should accept as historical the very minimum that the king might have achieved in order to make such claims. There are no complete inventions; something always occurred. Halpern calls it "minimal interpretation." In short, whatever the king could not plausibly lie about may be taken as having occurred. In his analysis of Sennacherib's campaign of 701, which included the siege of Jerusalem, Knauf (2003, 142) has added a second principle: what is *not* said may be as significant as what *is* said: bad news may simply be omitted. But let us bear in mind that we often cannot prove that these events did *not* occur even more or less as described; we can, however, sometimes deduce by comparing different accounts of the same royal campaigns in different inscriptions that these accounts were not always literally correct.

Assyrian annals, then, are not sober records of achievement, but a kind of literary version of the display inscription: they are as much for display as for reading, and they also serve to glorify or justify the king. Simultaneous events may appear as consecutive: in reality, campaigns could be carried out by divisions of the army at the same time (as probably occurred in 701). Numbers are often increased—including booty (and captives) taken, though the Assyrians very probably kept quite accurate records of such acquisitions. Annihilation of the (same) enemy can be achieved more than once.

In comparing these with biblical accounts, we are of course considering different genres. But the Judean reports obviously convey a Judean viewpoint. In almost any conflict, the two sides see and report things differently. Each account consists of propaganda, and in cases of discrepancy one, or quite probably all, are misleading. Where they agree, however, and precisely to the extent that they agree, we can reconstruct the events. Read as intended, inscriptions, like the biblical accounts, will tell us what the authors intended to convey. Where we have different versions of the same events, comparison allows us to detect the bias more easily. When we have only one version, we can bear in mind what we can learn from comparisons about the relationship between reality and representation. Therefore, we have to be very cautious in deciding how, or even if, the reported event occurred.

The inscriptions relating to biblical history have been collected and discussed many times and can easily be consulted. In the following review, which is in chronological sequence, we focus mainly on the difficulties that comparison of the biblical and non-biblical documents impose on the historian, and not on the history that might be derived from them.

Inscriptions Relating to Biblical History

The Merneptah Stele

Originally constructed by a predecessor, Amenhotep III, and inscribed later on the reverse, this is not just the earliest external source relevant to biblical history, but also the most curious. It was found in Merneptah's mortuary temple and celebrates victory in a campaign. After mentioning Canaan, and three Canaanite cities of Ashkelon, Gezer, and Yanoam, it runs, "Israel (?) is wasted, its seed is not." Assuming we have Merneptah's dates correctly as 1213–1203, and that the reading "Israel" is correct, the reference places an Israel in Palestine in the thirteenth century. The word read (probably correctly) as "Israel" also has a sign indicating a people and not a place. That makes the alternative reading "Jezreel" less likely—though Hebrew "s" and "z" could both be represented by the same Egyptian letter; also, since "Jezreel" is partly made up of the word for "seed," the inscription could be a pun by a Semitic-speaking scribe. It might also be considered that Merneptah would find it easier to fight in the plain of Jezreel than in the highlands. But although the vast majority of historians prefer the reading "Israel," we do not know what people "Israel" might be meant, and where they might be located. Two negative conclusions can be drawn. First, the claim that Israel was "laid waste" and "its seed is not" is obviously exaggerated, in the usual manner of ancient inscriptions—unless the name was subsequently adopted by another group later. Second, no such assault finds the slightest echo in any biblical account from Joshua, Judges, or Samuel. We cannot therefore reconstruct any event involving Israel from Merneptah's inscriptions. However, the positive inference is that the name "Israel" (if that is the correct reading) goes back at least to the end of the thirteenth century BCE.

Shalmaneser III and Sennacherib

More substantial issues are addressed by the inscriptions of Assyrian rulers describing conflicts between Assyria and Israel and Assyria and Judah (for a useful summary and evaluation, see Na'aman 1998). While many of them do confirm events related in the books of Kings, every one poses problems. The Kurkh stele (Monolith Inscription) of Shalmaneser III (859–842 BCE) records several campaigns in Syria and Palestine. In his sixth year (853), he fought a battle at Qarqar on the Orontes River in Syria against a coalition of kingdoms, led by Hadadezer of Aram and including Ahab the Israelite. Other inscriptions mention three later campaigns against the same forces. The problem for the historian in comparing these two Assyrian sources with the books of Kings arises not from the overlap between them but the lack of any biblical reference. The biblical stories of this period make no reference to the battle of Qarqar, any Assyrian threat, or any coalition with Aram. Instead, the reign of Ahab (2 Kgs. 6:12–22:40) is dominated by the confrontations with Elijah and wars with Aram (chaps. 20; 22). In the story of the final battle with Aram (chap. 22), the term "king of Israel" is used except for verse 20, and several scholars have suspected that the king in question was not Ahab, as that one reference claims, but Jehoram, Ahab's successor, and that Ahab died in battle against Assyria rather than Aram. It is not difficult to understand that a war *in alliance with* Aram and *against* Assyria would interfere with the plot of Ahab's reign, though the confusion, if such it is, could be the result of confusion rather than deliberate distortion. (In Na'aman's view the discrepancies are due to ignorance on the part of the later authors of the biblical narrative.) But to this confusion we can add a difference in the name of the Aramean king: Ben-Hadad in Kings and Hadad-ezer according to Shalmaneser. In Shalmaneser's Black Obelisk, which records a later campaign and depicts Jehu son of Omri doing obeisance, the Aramean king is called Hazael; again, the books of Kings make no mention of Shalmaneser, nor of Adad-nirari III (809–783), who claims to have mastered all of Syria and Palestine and to have received tribute from Joash the Samarian.

The events of 701 BCE—when Sennacherib invaded Judah, took Lachish and other Judean cities, besieged Jerusalem, and finally withdrew—are, however, detailed in Kings, and the whole episode analyzed many times (most recently in Grabbe 2003). There is no need to consider this story in detail. It provides another instance of broad agreement, though with many detailed factual discrepancies, complicated by the possibility that there are two biblical accounts that have later been combined. The Assyrian version, including the reliefs of the siege of Lachish from Sennacherib's palace, naturally focuses on glorifying Assyria and its king, and assumed a totally successful campaign. For the biblical account(s) the focus is on the fact that Jerusalem was not taken but miraculously saved, even though it is conceded that Hezekiah had to pay a large sum of money to Sennacherib.

The implication might be drawn from the biblical narrative that two separate campaigns were conducted, and some historians have concluded thus. But it is much more probable that we have simply two different stories in Kings of the same event (18:13–16, a short and rather factual account, and 18:17–19:37, a fuller and more obviously propagandistic version). The shorter version (if there are two of them) dates the event to Hezekiah's fourteenth year, which would be several years earlier. But there may be other calculations in effect: we have already seen the workings of biblical chronology in chapter 2. Otherwise, the major difference between the accounts is over whether Sennacherib was obliged to lift the siege hurriedly (thus in part vindicating the biblical spin) or had no interest in taking the city but only in reducing Hezekiah to submission (in line with the Assyrian spin). Perhaps both can be partly true. Unlike the instance discussed previously, there is pretty substantial agreement over what happened. The major lesson to be learned is, again, that the description of events in the recent past was dictated only partly by the course of the events themselves: more important were the requirements of the person or kingdom for which the account was written. The versions from each side tell us about the same event, but also about the perception, or rather the carefully constructed memory, of the event. That memory is, or should be, as valuable to the historian as the bare facts. But in identifying the ideology that informs ancient accounts, we had better bear in mind that our own version is not necessary ideology-free either! That is the nature of writing history, in any age.

Judah and the Neo-Babylonians

Similar issues are involved in comparing biblical and neo-Babylonian sources on the fall of Judah (detailed analysis in Lipschits 2005). Both mention the two invasions, in the first of which Jehoiachin was taken captive and several others also deported, and the second of which, ten years later, saw the city sacked and further deportation. Babylonian ideology was not identical to Assyrian, and the neo-Babylonian Chronicles offer a more sober and reliable genre of recording data. There are two major issues worth mentioning. One is the argument of 2 Kings (and Jeremiah) that Jerusalem fell because of the religious policies of its kings. The neo-Babylonians would have agreed that such things incurred divine anger, and the Assyrians would also. But ancient political treaties were also religious documents, and breaking them would in theory invoke divine retribution. The gods were routinely invoked as witnesses to treaties, and punishment of any breach, though inflicted by military might, would be justified in the name of these gods. The books of Kings present political relations in a slightly different way: Judah's disasters were punishments from its own god for offenses against the only treaty that matters: the one with Yhwh.

But the biblical versions on this occasion include the book of Jeremiah as well as 2 Kings, and there we find additional information about the aftermath not provided in Babylonian sources. The one other piece of information from Babylon is a ration list mentioning the king of Judah (Jehoiachin), confirming the final verse of 2 Kings—that he was treated well, as befitted a king who had, according to 2 Kings, ascended the throne only when the first invasion was already under way.

The Mesha Inscription

We can now turn to inscriptions from Palestine itself. Most Syro-Palestinian inscriptions can be classifed as either dedicatory or memorial: they mark, for example, the completion of a building or the offering of an object to a deity, or they serve to record the achievements of a ruler. In each case, as with Assyrian inscriptions, there are literary conventions to be followed (see Drinkard 1989). The stele erected by Mesha king of Moab (in ca. 830 BCE) is interesting partly because it shares a similar view of history with the books of Kings, with which its account overlaps. Mesha celebrates the making of a shrine for his god Kemosh in return for deliverance from "all the kings," and he proceeds to describe how Omri had oppressed his land for forty years (using good biblical chronology!). He then tells of his various successes against Israel and his rebuilding of a palace at Qarhoh. (For analyses of this text see Dearman [ed.] 1989; Routledge [2000] his written a very interesting analysis of the politics of the stele.)

The account has to be compared with the story in 2 Kings 3, according to which Mesha, who had been a vassal of Israel, rebelled. In response Jehoram of Israel and Jehoshaphat of Judah marched on Moab. Thanks to the intervention of Elisha, the army is initially successful, but when besieging Kir-hareseth, the king of Moab sacrificed his eldest son, "and great wrath came upon Israel, so they withdrew from him and returned to their own land" (v. 27). Here we can probably conclude with some confidence that Moab successfully rebelled against Israel, on which both sources agree (one implicitly). Mesha's reference to Omri might well mean just an Omride king and does not constitute a contradiction. But while Mesha makes no mention of Judah in his stele, 2 Kings 3 has Jehoram of Israel allied with Jehoshaphat of Judah. This matter is difficult to resolve: we might have expected Mesha to mention his defeat of Judah as well had it really been a kingdom allied with Israel. But there has in fact recently been a claim by André Lemaire (1994) that the name "David" occurs in the inscription. This is far from certain, though the word *dwdh* can be read elsewhere in this text. But we can deal with this issue when considering the Tel Dan inscription.

It should not be difficult to see that both accounts are structured according to different interests and conventions. Mesha wishes to magnify his own actions; the author of the Kings account wants to make a point about religion rather than war or politics. Thompson (2007) has suggested that because of its conventional structure and language, the Mesha inscription should not be regarded as evidence of any particular events, other than the building of the temple itself that occasioned it. But the reservation is not justified in this case. While some caution is always needed where we have only a single account, the presence of another, presumably independent version allows us to deduce that Moab had been a vassal of Israel and liberated itself—even if the details cannot be verified.

The Tel Dan Stele

The Tel Dan stele, discovered in two stages in 1993 and 1994, offers some degree of overlap with biblical accounts and has generated a good deal of controversy. We might begin with the unfortunate fact that the discovery of this stele, written in a dialect closer to Aramaic than Hebrew, and at the command of a king of Damascus/Aram, was not straightforward. A fragment was first found in a secondary location; then a second fragment also in a secondary location. The fragments have also been placed together, thus forming parts of a single inscription, by the editors in a way that has been challenged (there is no clear overlap between the two pieces). The genre of the inscription seems to be a victory stele (given that it was set up in the captured city) rather than a memorial inscription, though it has elements of the latter. The first fragment (A) of the inscription states that an (unnamed) king of Israel had invaded the territory of the father of the king responsible for the inscription, but that he had repulsed the invasion. Later there is a single word *bytdwd* that the editors (followed by the majority of scholars) read as "house of David"—corresponding to "house of Omri"—though their suggestion of a preceding *melek* ("king") would create a phrase unique in any ancient inscription or any biblical text. (No one was ever called "king of the house of Omri.") The name of a Judean king (Amaziah) is also supplied by the editors on the basis of the two final letters (the divine name *yh*).

But biblical correlations are again compromised by the fact that the implied historical scenario differs from the biblical one. If *bytdwd* refers to Judah, then perhaps the battle referred to is between Bar Hadad (Hebrew: Benhadad) II of Aram and Ahab of Israel allied with Jehoshaphat of Judah (1 Kgs. 22:29–38); or, in light of the editors' reading of the second fragment, between Hazael of Aram on one side and Joram of Israel allied with Ahaziah of Judah on the other (2 Kgs. 8:28–29; 9:14–16). But both battles took place, according to the Bible, at Ramoth Gilead in Transjordan, not near Dan. According to 1 Kings 15:16–22 (=2 Chron. 16:1–6) a battle did take place between Bar Hadad I of Aram and Baasha of Israel, in which Bar Hadad captured Dan, along with other Israelite cities. However, Asa the king of Judah was, according to this report, on the side of Bar Hadad against Baasha! Possibly the reference is to a battle that is not mentioned in 1 Kings. The existence of the stele confirms that the city of Dan was contested between Samaria and Damascus, but we cannot, from a comparison of the texts, be sure of the names of the protagonists, or the date of the event, if indeed the texts refer to a single event.

Much discussion of this stele has focused (see above) on the evidence for the existence of David in *bytdwd*. The word does not necessarily mean "house of David," and *dwd* is not a personal name: even applied to a king it must be some kind of title or nickname. Line 12 of the Mesha inscription contains the words, "I brought back from [Atarot] the '*r'l dwdh*," and if the final *he* of the second word is possessive, then we have *dwd* again, as in the Tel Dan inscription, as the second noun of a pair, in a possessive relationship. And Mesha's text can hardly mean "David." But Lemaire (1994) has since proposed that line 31 of Mesha's stele reads, "The house of David dwelt in Horonaim." The majority of scholars seem to doubt his reading, but in the present climate, when the very existence of David is being heatedly contested, opinions are sharply and predictably divided.

The Siloam Inscription

We consider last the most famous and, in the opinion of most people, the least problematic inscription from Judah. This was found in situ at the Siloam pool end of a tunnel running from the Gihon spring in the village of Silwan, where Iron Age Jerusalem stood. At some point in the past, this tunnel was attributed to Hezekiah, and the association has stuck. In favor of the identification with Hezekiah are comments in 2 Kings 20:20 and 2 Chronicles 32:3–4 that Hezekiah undertook waterworks in Jerusalem involving the Gihon spring. These mention a shaft and the stopping up of springs outside the city, but not specifically to a tunnel. Ben Sira, writing at the beginning of the second century BCE, also attributes to Hezekiah some waterworks involving excavation. Finally, Isaiah 22:9–11 (which might be dated to the time of Hezekiah) mentions the construction of a reservoir on the site of the "lower pool."

These references add up to a considerable degree of evidence connecting Hezekiah with providing water, utilizing the Gihon spring, and digging a conduit. By the time Kings and Chronicles were written, Hezekiah was perhaps already credited with such a system—and very reasonably, since the city was remembered as having been besieged in his day. It is also possible, as we have seen in the previous chapter, that the city underwent a large expansion in his time, and that the pool at the end of the tunnel may have now been inside the walls. But there are several systems connected to the Gihon spring (a shaft, a tunnel, and a channel), and the archaeology and architecture are complicated.

The inscription itself does not seem to have been known about, even in classical times—possibly because it was below water level (though its oversight still seems remarkable). There are photographs of it still in the tunnel, but it was removed soon after its discovery in 1880. It is unusual in having no formal traits of royal inscriptions and no royal name, and begins immediately with an account of how the tunnel was made without any formal opening. It uses the archaic script that was largely replaced in the fifth century BCE onward, but the script was revived (or perhaps never totally abandoned) in the Hasmonean era.

The suggestion (Rogerson and Davies 1996) that the tunnel and inscription might have been of Hasmonean date has been rejected by many, though without any decisive archaeological or epigraphic arguments. More recent archaeological work may resolve some of the claims, but the issue shows how fragile even a strong consensus can be, and the curiosities of the inscription remain unexplained. Clearly there is no question of a forgery, since the text does not claim any particular date, authorship, or historical context. But it is a puzzle, even if the majority of scholars do not seem inclined to raise questions about this most famous of biblical relics.

Forgeries

A word needs to be said about forgeries. Techniques of counterfeiting have, it seems, become extremely sophisticated, to the point where any unprovenanced item must be regarded with suspicion and ignored as historical evidence—simply because of doubt. Two instances of forgery can be mentioned. The first are seal impressions. Hundreds of bullae (pieces of hardened clay with a seal impression on them) have come to light during archaeological digs or in some other way during the last 150 years or so (see Avigad and

Sass 1997 for the entire corpus). During the 1970s, one inscribed with "Baruch" that was in the possession of a private collector was published: it reads: *lbrkyhw bn nryhw hspr* (belonging to Berechiah son of Neriah the scribe). Another had "belonging to Seraiah (ben) Neriah." Both characters are mentioned (if Berachiah=Baruch) in the book of Jeremiah. Either or both of these, and many others, could be fakes. Many are doubtless authentic. The problem is that not all fakes can necessarily be detected. Detecting *some* fakes does not prove that they can *all* be spotted. One criterion, of course, is that a seal with an unknown name is likely to be authentic: the main purpose of forgeries is to bolster support for biblical historicity. But in reality they actually achieve the opposite by undermining the possible value of a large number of authentic artifacts.

A second example of a forgery is the Joash inscription, which came to light in 2003. Again, it came to light from a private collection, and it claimed to be by the king himself. As such it would have been the first royal inscription from either Israel or Judah. On grounds of palaeography, orthography, and language as well as the condition of the tablet itself, it has been deemed a fake by most experts, including those of the Israel Antiquities Authority. The inscription describes repairs to the Jerusalem temple undertaken by the king from public donations. Such an event is narrated in 2 Kings 12:5–16 and 2 Chronicles 24:4–14. These reports could serve as the basis for the inscription, which adds no new information. But the only importance of such an inscription, if genuine, would be to help in confirming the reliability of the biblical account. As such it neither hinders nor assists the historian in any other way. Indeed, the damage done by such a forgery—or even a suspected forgery—is immeasurably greater than any benefit that might be derived were it to be genuine. In addition, the possible existence of a forgery industry at work somewhere in modern Israel is disturbing.

Summary

I have tried to show in this brief discussion how the third type of major historical source for the biblical historian requires careful and critical judgment. Unlike uninscribed artifacts, inscriptions are very often instruments of propaganda, and thus designed to convey an ideology, confirm a worldview, impart a spin—quite apart from misunderstandings that the modern interpreter may also bring to them. In most cases, unlike the biblical texts, we can confidently assign them a date and a place close to the events they describe. But they are still literary sources, and their testimony is not disinterested.

I have tried to show just how difficult it is for any historian to use such inscriptions to achieve historical results. Undoubtedly on the principle of independent attestation (see chap. 7) we can confirm the existence of several Israelite and Judean kings. We can confirm certain events. But there are also many cases where the accounts clearly have been manipulated, or that we cannot even reconstruct the event in question because of incompatibility between the differing versions. The biblical stories, in some cases, turn out to be unreliable, but this does not mean that the nonbiblical sources are necessarily more trustworthy. Fundamentally, we should be reminded that ancient accounts are, as we noted in chapter 2, less interested in facts than modern historians and are much more ready to make them fit the purpose for which they are inscribed and erected—that is, commemoration and self-glorification.

Conclusion to Part One

The previous chapters have shown, I hope, that none of the three sources of information about the past—Bible, archaeology, and inscriptions—is totally reliable. The Bible handles the past in ways that modern historians do not, and the modern concept of history as a critically derived account based on a concept of knowledge and respectful of chronology, fact, and causality is not part of its cultural horizon. Archaeology generates data that inform us a great deal about material culture, but extrapolating particular events, and even constructing firm chronologies, is a matter of interpretation and sometimes conjecture. It is here in particular that "fact" and "data" have to be very carefully distinguished. Inscriptions, though they usually refer to specific historical events, are created largely for the purposes of propaganda and inform us as much about the ideology of their creators as about the events. They are capable, like the biblical narratives, of relating accurate accounts, distorted accounts, or even invented accounts.

None of the three sources provides an ideal foundation for the construction of a modern history. The task is easiest where more than one source can attest to the same events or condition, and we can at least infer the existence of whatever the accounts refer to. But we cannot always reconstruct the details; it is usually easier to recognize the bias of each source. The history that we want to recover—a reliable sequence of known facts (or rather, what passes in history for knowledge)—falls between these three, none of which is either concerned or competent to provide that knowledge.

Of the three sources of data, the Bible is the fullest and has until now provided the foundation for every history of Israel. But as a historical source it is of equal, or even greater, use to the historian as a clue to the historical contexts in which its stories arose. In any case, without some notion of where and when and why these stories were produced, we are even less capable of assessing the value of what they claim for the past.

In recognizing the virtues and limitations of the "traces of the past in the present," the historian may still be unable to write a really good history. But at least a number of bad ones can be avoided.

References

Avigad, Nahman, and Benjamin Sass
   1997   *Corpus of West Semitic Stamp Seals*, Jerusalem: Israel Academy of Sciences and Humanities.

Dearman, J. Andrew (ed.)
   1989   *Studies in the Mesha Inscription and Moab*, Atlanta: Scholars Press.

Drinkard, Joel
   1989   "The Literary Genre of the Mesha Inscription," in Dearman (ed.), 132–54.

Grabbe, Lester L. (ed.)
   2003   *"Like a Bird in a Cage": The Invasion of Sennacherib in 701 BCE*, London: Sheffield Academic Press.

Halpern, Baruch
    2001   *David's Secret Demons: Messiah, Murderer, Traitor, King*, Grand Rapids:
           Eerdmans.

Knauf, E. Axel
    2003   "Sennacherib at the Berezina," in Grabbe (ed.), 141–49.

Lemaire, André
    1994   "'House of David' Restored in Moabite Inscription," *Biblical Archaeology
           Review* 20:31–37.

Lipschits, Oded
    2005   *The Fall and Rise of Jerusalem*, Winona Lake, Ind.: Eisenbrauns.

Millard, Alan R.
    1972   "The Practice of Writing in Ancient Israel," *Biblical Archaeologist*
           35:98–111.

Na'aman, Nadav
    1998   "The Contribution of Royal Inscriptions for a Re-Evaluation of the Book
           of Kings as a Historical Source," *Journal for the Study of the Old Testament*
           82:3–17.

Rogerson, John W., and Philip R. Davies
    1996   "Was the Siloam Tunnel Built by Hezekiah?" *Biblical Archaeologist*
           59:138–49.

Routledge, Bruce
    2000   "The Politics of Mesha: Segmented Identities and State Formation in
           Iron Age Moab," *Journal of the Economic and Social History of the Orient*
           43:221–56.

Thompson, Thomas L.
    2007   "Mesha and Questions of Historicity," *Scandinavian Journal of the Old Tes-
           tament* 21:241–60.

Part Two

Strategies

Chapter Six

Cultural Memory

In this section of the book we turn to conceptual and methodological issues. While there is much to be said for ad hoc judgments, taking individual cases on merit, such a procedure cannot
provide an excuse for avoiding questions of method and presup-
position. All historians write within a historical and cultural context, and with a view of what writing history means and entails. It
is worth making these explicit. In any case, biblical history is not
on the whole conducive to ad hoc judgments because the literature itself is anonymous, of uncertain date, and for the most part
unconfirmed. Without some general perception of what this literature is, how its relationship to the past should be understood,
and how it should be classified and treated, the historian will
accomplish no more than making subjective guesses.

I deal with matters of knowledge, judgment, and belief in the
next chapter. But first I think it necessary to form an understanding of how we should broadly classify the biblical literature.
I want to suggest a conceptual model that will provide a platform
for our judgments research; it involves a more precise, less
ambiguous redescription of ancient writing about the past not as
history, but *memory*.

On Remembering History

History turns into myth as soon as it is remembered, narrated
and used, that is, woven into the fabric of the present.

Seen as an individual and as a social capacity, memory is
not simply the storage of past "facts" but the ongoing work
of reconstructive imagination. In other words, the past cannot be stored but always has to be "processed" and mediated.

(Assmann 1997, 14)

What is more important about the past than facts? The answer is
memory, because memory, whether personal or collective,
belongs to us. It is our history. Nor is it a disinterested recollection, but something basic to our identity and our future. Our
memory of what we have experienced enables us at each moment
to sustain identity. Total amnesia is a total loss of self. We are,
except in a purely biological sense, what we remember.

This is true for both individuals and groups. Personal and collective memory work not only analogically but cooperatively.
Maurice Halbwachs, from whom most modern discussion of collective memory stems, was a follower of Emile Durkheim, whose
sociological theory stressed the role of the collective in the shap-
ing of personal identity. Halbwachs (1992) argues that individual
memory itself was not possible outside a social context, that one
actually remembers only what one communicates and what one
can localize within the frame of reference of collective memory.

That may be an extreme formulation, but individual identity at
any rate is meaningless without the existence of other identities
from which it can be differentiated. But identity is created by
memory through interpreting the past as a coherent narrative, or
set of narratives. It is not a receptacle of meaningless recollections,
but it selects and edits. Here the analogy with history is immediate; history is not merely a recollection of facts but a narrative of
facts, a meaningful conjunction. The writing of history, whether
ancient or modern, is an act of recollection, and produces what is,
in form, a collective memory of the past. However, Halbwachs
very clearly distinguished modern critical history-writing from
cultural "memorizing." The historian is, among other things, a

historian of cultural memory itself, concerned to show how what is recollected about the past changes with the collective identity itself, adapting the past to the present.

The terms "cultural," "social," and "collective" memory are all used for group recollection. I have opted for "cultural memory" because this seems the name that is being mostly adopted in biblical scholarship. Moreover, it does not include only collective memory but also personal. The individual's own memory is partly composed of a social layer, just as an individual's personal identity also has components of the identities of groups (families, classes, gangs, professions, nationalities) to which each individual belongs.

Cultural memory can perhaps best be explained further by means of an illustration that explains the social and personal overlap. Although I am not personally religious, I still feel culturally and personally deprived at Christmas without carols, without hearing the story of the birth in Bethlehem, the journey of the wise men. It is not that I have a religiosity that I am trying to deny; nor that I really believe in the historicity of these stories. (In fact, my knowledge that they are probably legendary does not affect my enjoyment at all—though it might affect the enjoyment of others.) My feelings are not, I think, merely nostalgic or sentimental, evocative of past childhood or adolescent Christmases. The annual repetition of the festival is undoubtedly a powerful cultural marker of the cyclic time that we all experience, and each Christmas is more easily comparable (i.e., linked in memory) to other Christmases of the past than to the days or weeks preceding the festival. But there is at the core an archetype, the story of the first "Christmas," and this story is part of my cultural memory. For Jews, the Passover Seder works in perhaps an even stronger way as a cultural memorial of the archetypal event, the exodus. These are not memories in the sense of recollections of things experienced, but they are stories about the past that are recollected, and which serve to reinforce group identity, including the individual identities of members of the group. In the case of Christmas, the group includes worshiping Christian believers but a wider group, embracing also many nonbelievers and half-believers.

But what history am I remembering at Christmas? The actual events? No. The Christmas story of my cultural memory, as with everyone else, is of a midwinter night, a stable, shepherds, three kings, a massacre of children by Herod. This is certainly not the biblical Christmas, which in fact contains two stories, one in Matthew and one in Luke. Neither Gospel indicates the season of the year, and the fact that the sheep are in the fields at night (Luke only) may suggest that the evangelist did not think of midwinter. In any case, we know (or can find out) that the midwinter date of Christmas was fixed by Dionysius Exiguus, a Russian monk, in the mid-sixth century. (Dionysius's argument was apparently based on a date of conception of March 25, believed to be the day on which the world was created.) However, either by remarkable coincidence or as the result of additional reasoning this date coincided with the Roman midwinter festival of Saturnalia, or the birth of Sol Invictus (the rebirth of the Sun)—and with every other midwinter festival in the northern hemisphere. Hence holly, ivy, yule logs, and Christmas trees have been incorporated into the celebration, not to mention St. Nicholas, whose feast day of December 6 is near enough to move and who has morphed into Santa Claus or Father Christmas. The feast of the Epiphany on January 6 (which is also the eve of the Orthodox Christmas) celebrates the arrival of the Magi, who are often remembered as having been at the crib with the shepherds two weeks earlier. But neither Matthew nor Luke mentions ox or ass. The Magi were not described by Matthew as kings, nor was it said how many, let alone their names. While Herod and Quirinius both existed, the reign of Herod and the census of Quirinius cannot be correlated to give a birth date. The massacre of the innocents reads suspiciously like the story of the birth of Moses, and such a momentous event is curiously missing from any other ancient account of Herod's life. And did Mary and Joseph previously live in Nazareth (Luke), or did they migrate there later to escape Herod's rule? Matthew takes the family to Egypt; Luke has the boy presented in the temple, under Herod's nose. They cannot both be right.

Christmas illustrates three different levels of history and memory. The modern memory of Christmas is a mixture of two partly contradictory and probably legendary biblical narratives plus a great deal of later embellishment; the narratives relate a birth that took place, but under what circumstances we cannot now really know.

Imagine a culture in which most remembrance of the past is like this, where we do not have historians to point out where and how the various components really originated, where the story of the Nativity would be indistinguishable from history. Early Judaism celebrated its past publicly in festivals that had each their own story: exodus for Passover, lawgiving for Weeks/Pentecost, wilderness wandering for Booths/Tabernacles. Like midwinter Christmas, these festivals occur at times of the year that carry additional significance, for all coincide with key moments in the life of the farmer: the birthing of lambs, and the harvests of cereal and fruit, that enhance their significance. In addition, Purim and Hanukkah celebrate the story of Esther and the rededication of the temple in 163 BCE. Apart from the very last of these, we really cannot affirm that any of the events celebrated actually took place. But if they did, the memory is not direct, but has been inherited, and in the process accumulated embellishments and rituals. To put it bluntly: the shape and survival of Judaism over the last two millennia owes very little to whatever history lies behind the biblical narrative, but a great deal to the telling of stories about that past (and the adaptation of its laws into codes for a decentralized and noncultic way of life). This persistence of cultural memory has sustained Jewish identity, and as such it sustains secular as well as religious Jews in the same way that Christmas also sustains those of a Christian culture but not Christian belief.

Applying these illustrations to biblical history, we can therefore usefully consider three distinct stages of cultural memorizing that have provided the sense of the past. The first is that of the various Israels and inner-Israel groups that nurtured their own histories. The second is the achievement of the biblical writers, whose stories no doubt partly drew on these existing memories but compiled them into continuous narratives which presented a combined history of a combined Israel that incorporated several Israels into a single nation. It also excluded some Israels (in Samaria). This memory was later canonized. The final stage is achieved by modern historians who receive these memories. But they are received in two ways: as part of the cultural memory of modern Christendom but also a story about a past whose reality it is the historian's business to reconstruct. They are memory but a memory subject to critical review. Unlike earlier generations, the modern historian does not, and cannot equate this memory with history, since "history" has been redefined as an account of real events, real knowledge. We might say that the birth of modern critical history is the birth of a new kind of professional, secular, cultural memory, and that view could be defended, for written cultural memories—this is a very important point—are the product of individuals and small groups, not of society at large. But while the historian can see cultural memory and history as distinct, nonhistorians sometimes confuse the two, seeing the biblical memory as historical memory. This confusion is deepened in cases where religious believers require the Bible's memory to be historically accurate, and thus believe that their own cultural memory is not like others, but sober fact. But it is understandable, for critical historical reconstruction lacks the persuasive and emotional power of cultural memory in providing existential meaning, reinforcing identity and values and illuminating trajectories toward the future. Modern history, the history of a shared human past, belongs in principle to everyone, and so to no one in particular. In practice, as I argued in chapter 1, even critical histories cannot achieve this ideal and in fact cannot avoid expressing cultural values and prejudices. But they generally do so innocently or by default, whereas the purpose of cultural memory is precisely not to record, but to remember, with everything that the act of remembering entails.

Contemporary cultural memory is something that the historian has to confront, both positively and negatively. Negatively, it has to be interrogated concerning its claims about the past, not merely repeated. But cultural memory has its own history, and that is part of the modern historian's remit. Cultural memories have a life of their own. In the last few decades, biblical scholarship has become more and more interested in reception, the way in which the Bible and its texts have been read, used, and passed on. Such studies reveal the fascinating interplay of a (more or less) stable set of words and an evolving culture in which their meaning is given (or taken). Paradoxically, it is precisely this history of reception that the modern biblical historian is trying to filter out in aiming for the original event or episode or person, the past as it was; yet the Bible, the most important human product of Palestine's ancient past, is itself a repository of memory, and the history of the production of the Bible is a history of the evolution of ancient Judean memory. The modern biblical historian is thus inevitably a historian of cultural memory.

The Bible as Judean Cultural Memory

The phenomenon of cultural memory is only just being introduced into biblical scholarship. The credit for this belongs chiefly to the Egyptologist Jan Assmann and his book on Moses (1997). Here Assmann is interested in Western civilization's cultural memories of the Bible and of Egypt, but he draws attention to the value of the concept as a tool for explaining and analyzing biblical history writing. Others have long used the notion of memory, explicitly or implicitly, as a way of pleading for the essential reliability of the biblical stories. One scholar to have seriously taken up the notion of biblical narrative as cultural memory is Mark Smith (2004), who quite deliberately adopts cultural memory as a definition of the biblical account of the past. Cultural memory is, however, also being used by others as a more modern-sounding term for tradition, and Smith himself still operates within a classical source- and redaction-critical model that does not seem to make the distinction as crucial as it needs to be in order to allow for the critical notion of memory as capable of invention and not just distortion. Brettler (2003), on the other hand, is quite explicit in his demonstration that the past can be created. The basic notion of *traditio* is of a "handing on" (so the German word *Überlieferung*), a continuity. The word easily lends itself to belief in an essential and perhaps recoverable core of history, despite the well-known and well-documented phenomenon of invented tradition (for which, see Lewis and Hammer 2007). Such continuity may seem to sustain a link, however fragile, between a real past and a story about it. But cultural memory does not necessarily preserve links. It can effect quite sharp breaks, especially—as in human memory—in cases of trauma. The story comes to mind of the woodsman and the axe that had been in his family for generations: it had acquired several new handles and several new blades, but was still the same old axe, as good as new. The point is not that cultural memory has no true recollection, but that true recollection is not intrinsic to its mechanism or its purpose: equally important are inventing and forgetting.

Assmann's use of "myth" invokes the popular opposition of myth and history as "untrue" and "true." But this is not his meaning; or at least I do not think it is. Rather, "history" means the simple facts, things that really happened, while "myth" means a narrative that creates an understanding of the world as it is experienced, including politics, human nature, and ethics. The notion of cultural memory lies precisely between the two. It is myth in the sense just defined, but in the form of history as just defined. It is a category that explodes the distinction—which is a modern distinction anyway and inappropriate for text from the first millennium. We can remind ourselves that there is no clear point where the biblical narrative switches from one to the other (or rather, would seem to us to switch).

We have seen earlier in this book examples of forgetfulness on the part of the Bible: how Joshua's conquest was somehow undone, how the kingdom of Judah came into being alongside Saul's Israel, how Benjamin came to ally itself with Judah, events in the "empty land" of the neo-Babylonian period, and the ongoing "Israel" of Samaria, while examples of creativity were given in chapter 2. How are such things achieved? It is often protested that invention or distortion of the past cannot take place because people know what happened and will not tolerate distortion, invention, or forgetting. This is clearly wrong: during my own lifetime I have seen how memories of the Second World War in the West "forget" the role of the Russians, while Hollywood reminds a generation with no direct experience of the war that America won it alone. Popular memory is very easily manipulated, especially when the created memory is preferable. In the ancient Middle East, royal and priestly control of state ideology was probably quite effective and the production of official memories even easier than today. Cultural memory exists for groups and classes as well as whole societies, and on various levels the production of new "memories" is quite easy. But the practice is not to be deplored: revising the past is precisely what memory does, and the need to adjust one's perception in order to sustain a stable identity is strong.

The introduction of writing endowed cultural memory with a new power. As Assmann notes (1992, 23), "Only with writing in the strict sense can the external domain of communication become self-aware and complex." It can also to some extent protect its content from the invisible evolution of orally communicated memory. But texts can of course be edited. The stories in the Bible are not to be equated with the folk memories of Israel or Judah. We do not know, except by deduction, what these memories were. Literacy is a professional skill, and the writing and reading of literature were confined to the scribal class, who were part of the apparatus of state administration, economically and ideologically. They did not write paperbacks for mass consumption. If not exactly working for Orwell's famous Ministry of Truth, they served just the same function in what was a totalitarian polity. The stories that they told were, in any case, fed and absorbed into the public memory, through public recitation, by word of mouth, and ultimately by formal instruction and by being adopted into popular liturgy. In medieval Europe, the populace, while aware vaguely of the contents of the Bible, did not (indeed, were not allowed to) read the Bible, but heard it from the religious authorities and saw it performed liturgically and dramatically. Cultural memory may in theory function autonomously, but it is generally prompted by social, political, and religious agencies. If the mechanisms that control memory in individual humans are the domain of psychology and physiology, those that control the memory of human groups are for the sociologist—and the historian.

Cultural memory is neither coherent nor monolithic. This too is the case with human memory. Our memory comprises discrete recollections, not a single coherent narrative. Identities, personal and social, are multilayered. Connecting them up has to be done consciously, and assembling discrete memories is one way of influencing them, imposing a grander structure upon them. Within the extended biblical narratives of the past we can find clear traces of distinct and contradictory memories, especially about the origins of the nation. There are stories from Israel and from Judah, from various sanctuaries and tribal areas, and even from different scribal schools. These stories reflect different identities, including different Israels: the combined narrative creates an overarching Israelite identity from these, but without obscuring them.

One of the clearest modern accounts of Judean cultural memory is provided by Mario Liverani (2005), though he does not use the term. His portrayal of Israel's history is divided into two distinct sections: a "normal" history, in which Israel is presented as one of a number of nations that flourished between two "caesuras"—the breakdown of society at the end of the Late Bronze Age that gave rise to new kinds of social formation—and the end of a certain kind of imperial politics that in the sixth century gave way to new forms of religion and governance. This Israel is not historically remarkable, and does not of itself justify the enormous attention paid to it by comparison to its neighbors. What does make it remarkable is the Bible. For Liverani, the Bible represents (among other things) an "invented history," which he analyzes in the second part of his book. This "invented history" consists of several strands, all of which can be traced to the immigrants who came to Judah, mostly from Babylonia, in the late sixth century onward, the self-styled "returnees" from "exile." Their identity vis-à-vis the "remainees" who had never left the land, or who had immigrated during the previous century, is negotiated through various narratives of the past. One such narrative is of conquest, to which Liverani links the stories of exodus and wilderness wanderings. This narrative manifests a strategy of forcibly removing indigenous populations and is coupled with a very ambitious, utopian definition of the extent of the promised land. The narratives of the ancestors, by contrast, express a more integrative vision of peaceful immigration and settlement. The narrative of the Judges period is invented for a nation without a king, that of the united monarchy by those who still yearned for a return to kingship—an incipient messianic hope—while the Solomonic temple is an invention of the priestly caste. The law embedded in the combined narrative constitutes an exercise in self-identity of the immigrant group.

Liverani's separation of the various strategies is open to challenge on many details. But his scheme offers an effective means of separating a modern critical account of Israelite and Judean history from the biblical narrative. It avoids the difficulty of paraphrasing or modifying the canonized story into a modern history, but integrates the two by fitting the "invented history" within the "normal history" by attaching its various episodes and strands to specific groups in a specific historical context. In *The Origins of Biblical Israel* (2007), I have concentrated on the definitions of "Israel" that emerge from the various strands of cultural memory and broadened the authorship of these memories beyond the immigrant groups. Hence, biblical Israel—which, as was demonstrated in chapter 3, is not a stable construct in the biblical narratives—is therefore a product of combined and negotiated cultural memories, of identity claiming, and not even a given datum of normal history. The process did not cease in the act of canonization: the role of memory in Jewish (as well as Christian and pagan) identity building in the Hellenistic period has been explored by Doron Mendels (1992, 2004), and Mendels has continued to develop his interest in the comparative study of memory (2007). The issue remaining, and likely to be debated ad infinitum, is just how much of these memories is indeed genuine recollection and can be converted into our notion of history, and how much is not. And how far can we actually decide, either way?

Cultural Memory in Practice: Ezra and Nehemiah

The contrast between history and cultural memory, and the correspondingly different way of analyzing biblical narrative, can be illustrated by the case of Ezra and Nehemiah. Because we have little or no alternative account of the events of this period, it has been (and by and large still is) the norm to take these books as a basically reliable account of what actually happened. But the difficulties of conventional historical reconstruction are well known. The two stories seem to be narrating many of the same processes: it is not clear how Nehemiah's and Ezra's offices and tasks were differentiated and why both were apparently authorized by the Persian authorities to operate in Judah. They appear to be contemporary, though it is unclear, since the Persian king Artaxerxes in question is not identified, whether the two really were contemporary or if Ezra came first—and if his mission was therefore a failure, requiring Nehemiah to make a second attempt at preventing, say, intermarriage.

There are further problems with the temple building. In Ezra 3 the altar is built and in use, and the temple foundations laid. According to Ezra 4:24 it was stopped under Artaxerxes, who came to the throne in 464. But it is finished (Ezra 6:15) "in the sixth year of the reign of King Darius" and "by decree of Cyrus, Darius, and King Artaxerxes." But by the time of Artaxerxes, under whom both Ezra and Nehemiah serve, the temple is already built! The chronological setting is further complicated by Nehemiah's complaint to Artaxerxes at the start of the book that "the survivors there in the province who escaped captivity are in great trouble and shame; the wall of Jerusalem is broken down, and its gates have been destroyed by fire" (1:3). This can hardly refer to a land already reoccupied by returnees over the preceding century following the fall of Babylon. He seems to be saying that the city is as the Babylonians had left it in 586 (and admitting that there were Judeans who were not deported!). There is a gap of about a century between the announcement of Cyrus and the work of the two men: what really happened in that time?

A different kind of problem is the trajectory implied by these books, of an exclusive temple-bound community in conflict with Samaria, and rejecting the people of the land does not make sense in light of what we know from other sources about the evolution of Judaism and Samari(t)anism in Palestine. Typologically the stories indicate an increasingly exclusive definition of the new Israel. Finally, there is the problem that while Nehemiah is mentioned in later Jewish literature, and with additional details (Ben Sira 49:13 and 2 Macc. 1:18–36; 2:13), he is mentioned without Ezra;

and indeed Ezra is completely disregarded in any other source until the first century CE (for a good analysis of all these issues, see Grabbe 1998).

These problems can be partly solved by suggesting that the books of Ezra and Nehemiah began as independent stories, but were later combined. The overlapping of genealogical lists, and the bringing together of both characters in one central scene of Nehemiah 8–9 (or 8–10) would be the major outcome of such an exercise. Hence, the two characters need not have met historically and their missions can be regarded as distinct. Indeed, while Nehemiah has no place in the book of Ezra, Ezra is mentioned four times—but only incidentally—in Nehemiah 12, once as "the priest Ezra, the scribe" (v. 26) and once as "the scribe Ezra" (v. 36). A case could therefore be made even that Ezra was fashioned from this minor character, as a counterpart to Nehemiah. But it is hard to see why this should have been done. The suggestion that Ezra and Nehemiah were originally the heroes of initially independent accounts would explain many of the problems of the combined books. However, it still leaves a major problem, which is either to fit both characters into the history of Persian-era Judah without any overlap or to accept that one or the other is not a historical character. There is in fact no satisfactory historical reconstruction of the contents of the Ezra–Nehemiah narrative.

Let us now try and analyze the stories as products of cultural memory, starting from the conclusion that the Ezra and Nehemiah accounts were originally independent of each other. We have, accordingly, two memories of the birth of a new society, and two founders. One is a layman, whose aims were to restore Jerusalem and repopulate it—also to secure the community against outsiders, partly by strengthening social boundaries and partly by increasing internal cohesion through the imposition of such rules as Sabbath observance. The other founder is a priest and scribe whose mission focuses on the adoption of the law of Moses and a new pledge by all the people to observe it. The language and ideology of Ezra are reminiscent of Deuteronomy, and Ezra seems to be understood as a second Moses. These characterizations would suggest, incidentally, that the contents of Nehemiah 8–10 belonged originally with the Ezra story, and that in all probability Ezra 1–6 belonged originally to neither story but was added later, possibly when the figures of Ezra and Nehemiah were brought together. These chapters connect Ezra and Nehemiah with other stories of the return that featured Haggai and Zechariah, Zerubbabel and Sheshbazzar, and in doing so create long-standing problems of historical reconstruction of that return, including having to distance both characters by several decades from the first initiatives—making them quite belated "founders." Yet Nehemiah 1:1–3, as just observed, implies that he undertook his mission with the city still devastated.

The existence of two independent memories of how the new Israel began implies two groups, each having its identity and interests reflected in the profile of its hero and his achievements. The union of the two stories implies that these groups merged their memories into a single memory—or that their memories were merged for them!—resulting in a single memory of how Judaism began. The attaching of Ezra 1–6, if this was also part of an editorial process, cements that unified story to the wider story of an edict from Cyrus, though it also complicates the portrait of a mass return. In short, the literary history of the books reflects very vividly a process of remembering and re-remembering by two Jewish groups.

The exclusivist tendencies in Ezra and Nehemiah—which, as observed, do not fit with other indications of how Judaism developed in Palestine in the Persian era—make better sense from this perspective, because the existence of more than one group within Judean society implies the possibility of sectarian characteristics in which those outside each group might (but would not necessarily) include other Judeans. We have plenty of evidence from the Dead Sea Scrolls and possibly also the Enochic literature that such groups did exist; indeed, the *Damascus Document* contains a story quite similar to that of Ezra, with an anonymous hero called the "Interpreter of the Law." This Damascus group also sees itself as the remnant of old Israel that had been into exile. Indeed, tracing origins back to exile seems to be a common denominator of all three stories, implying a common memory that "all Israel" had been taken into exile and that only those who returned constituted legitimate descendants. The self-designation "children of the *golah* [exile]" occurs several times in Ezra and once in Nehemiah, while the Qumran *Damascus Document* uses the designation *šby ysr'l*, (returners/captivity of Israel) of the group that it represents.

This analysis (given in more detail in Davies 1995) makes a different kind of history out of Ezra–Nehemiah, and one that I suggest explains the characteristic of these books better than a conventional historical reconstruction. Indeed it is possible to extract a fuller history. The anti-Samaritan and pro-Jerusalem stance of his story implies political as well as religious opposition between Jerusalem and Samaria. At the beginning of the second century BCE, Ben Sira (50:26) alludes to "the foolish people that live in Shechem," a likely reference to Samari(t)ans and their temple on Mount Gerizim. In 107 BCE the Judean king and high priest John Hyrcanus destroyed that temple, definitively making the "Israelite" religion of Palestine a Judean one; thereafter we can quite correctly speak of "Judaism" in this sense. Nehemiah's story belongs somewhere in this trajectory.

We can actually see the memory of Nehemiah developing outside the book bearing his name. (The stories about Nehemiah in 2 Maccabees have been addressed by Bergren [1997], though he assumes that the canonical books of Ezra and Nehemiah were already well-known and so concludes that the stories are manufactured by the author.) By the first century BCE, the writer of 2 Maccabees states (1:18–36):

> Since on the twenty-fifth day of Chislev we shall celebrate the purification of the temple, we thought it necessary to notify you, in order that you also may celebrate the festival of booths and the festival of the fire given when Nehemiah, who built the temple and the altar, offered sacrifices. But after many years had passed, when it pleased God, Nehemiah, having been commissioned by the king of Persia, sent the descendants of the priests who had hidden the fire to get it. And when they reported to us that they had not found fire but only a thick liquid, he ordered them to dip it out and bring it. When the materials for the sacrifices were presented, Nehemiah ordered the

priests to sprinkle the liquid on the wood and on the things laid upon it. And while the sacrifice was being consumed, the priests offered prayer—the priests and everyone. Jonathan led, and the rest responded, as did Nehemiah. After the materials of the sacrifice had been consumed, Nehemiah ordered that the liquid that was left should be poured on large stones. When this matter became known, and it was reported to the king of the Persians that, in the place where the exiled priests had hidden the fire, the liquid had appeared with which Nehemiah and his associates had burned the materials of the sacrifice, Nehemiah and his associates called this "nephthar," which means purification, but by most people it is called naphtha.

Not only is Nehemiah here credited with building the temple, but Ezra is entirely absent. Later the author writes (2:13), "The same things are reported in the records and in the memoirs of Nehemiah, and also that he founded a library and collected the books about the kings and prophets, and the writings of David, and letters of kings about votive offerings."

But if we can trace the growing memory of Nehemiah before it was combined with that of Ezra, can we conclude that such a person might have existed? It is interesting that part of the book of Nehemiah is cast in the first person: many critics indeed speak therefore of "Nehemiah's memoir," and regard its contents as contemporary with the events and therefore reliable. Such a conclusion casts further doubt on the historicity of Ezra. But the logic can work both ways. If the book of Nehemiah contains a genuine memoir, then its account of the political and religious situation reflects fifth-century realities after all. Or, if the portrait of the situation is improbable and fits a later period better, then the memoir is *not* a true one, and we have a cultural memory in the form of a fictive autobiography (we might compare parts of the book of Daniel, especially chap. 4).

Ezra's story presents him as instating the law at the center of Israel's life. We know of later Jewish groups for whom exact obedience to the law defined Judaism: Pharisees, *haverim*, who enjoined levitical purity at their everyday meals; the keepers of the Qumran scrolls, the author of the book of Jubilees—and the rabbis, of course. Intermarriage with foreigners is also a prominent issue among certain Jewish groups in the late Second Temple period, perhaps responding negatively to the enlargement of the Jewish nation under the Hasmoneans by the incorporation of Idumea, Galilee, and other territory to the Judean kingdom. Indeed, that political act may have followed a prolonged period during which the cult of Yahweh spread through Palestine and even beyond, creating a large and varied "Jewish" population. The memory of Ezra, at any rate, can be traced in 1 Esdras, Josephus, and 4 Ezra. First Esdras is generally regarded as an expansion of the book of Ezra and the last two chapters of Chronicles, including two additional stories in chapters 3–4. This is the source that Josephus uses in his *Jewish Antiquities*, but unfortunately, we have no reliable clues about the origin or date of this work. More or less contemporary with Josephus, at the end of the first century BCE, stands 4 Ezra, in which the hero restores the lost books of Scripture (and other books)—perhaps challenging the story in 2 Maccabees (see above) about Nehemiah and *his* work in gathering books for a library. The origin and growth of the Ezra memory is therefore harder to date: although three small fragments from the book were found at Qumran, dating from the first century BCE (and, incidentally, nothing from the book of Nehemiah), they are from chapters 4–6, in which Ezra does not appear at all. If Ezra 1–6 contains stories added to the Ezra–Nehemiah story at some point, these fragments tell us nothing useful about the memory of Ezra. So is Ezra a real historical figure? The case seems on the one hand weaker than Nehemiah's, since we have no other trace of an early memory. On the other hand, the lists in Nehemiah 12 do mention an Ezra. The issue is whether these lists are names of returnees from Babylon or lists of members of the groups that remembered Ezra or Nehemiah in a later period.

If the reader is thinking that cultural memory is a way of minimalizing history, then this is misguided. The problems of a conventional historical reconstruction exist regardless and are not created by applying the concept of cultural memory: in fact, they become rather easier to solve. Moreover, we can gain a great deal of history, not just of a different kind but perhaps also more reliable.

Summary

Cultural memory provides a better conceptual tool than history, myth, or tradition for classifying the biblical narratives about the past because it better reflects the ways in which the past was understood and utilized in ancient societies. Regarding the biblical narratives as a Judean collection of cultural memories, integrated into continuous accounts, enables the historian to understand better the problems that they raise for conventional historical reconstruction but also sheds more light on the history behind these memories and their literary production. In particular, accepting that cultural memory—like personal memory—not only recalls the past but also forgets and invents it severs the notion of a necessary link between historical event and narrative account. Finally, focusing on the purpose for which the past is recalled, forgotten, or created rather than on its historical reliability provides a means whereby these memories can be treated as an important part of the cultural history of ancient Israel and Judah.

References

Assmann, Jan
   1992, 1999   *Das kulturelle Gedächtnis: Schrift, Erinnerung und politische Identität in frühen Hochkulturen*, Munich: Beck.

   1997   *Moses the Egyptian: The Memory of Egypt in Western Monotheism*. Cambridge, Mass., and London: Harvard University Press.

   2006   *Religion and Cultural Memory: Ten Studies*, trans. Rodney Livingstone, Stanford, Calif.: Stanford University Press.

Bergren, Theodore A.
   1997   "Nehemiah in 2 Maccabees 1:10–2:18," *Journal for the Study of Judaism in the Persian, Hellenistic, and Roman Periods* 28 (1997): 249–70.

Brettler, Marc Zvi
   2003   *The Creation of History in Ancient Israel*, London: Routledge.

Davies, Philip R.
   1995 "Scenes from the Early History of Judaism," in D. V. Edelman (ed.), *The Triumph of Elohim*, Kampen: Kok Pharos, 145–82.
   2007 *The Origins of Biblical Israel*, London: T&T Clark.

Grabbe, Lester L.
   1998 *Ezra-Nehemiah*, London: Routledge.

Halbwachs, Maurice
   1992 *On Collective Memory* (ed. and trans. Lewis A. Coser), Chicago: University of Chicago Press (original *Les cadres sociaux de la mémoire*, Paris: F. Alcan, 1925).

Lewis, James R., and Olav Hammer (eds.)
   2007 *The Invention of Sacred Tradition*, Cambridge: Cambridge University Press.

Liverani, Mario
   2005 *Israel's History and the History of Israel*, London: Equinox.

Mendels, Doron
   1992 *The Rise and Fall of Jewish Nationalism: Jewish and Christian Ethnicity in Ancient Palestine*, Grand Rapids: Eerdmans.

   2004 *Memory in Jewish, Pagan, and Christian Societies of the Graeco-Roman World*, London: T&T Clark.

Mendels, Doron (ed.)
   2007 *On Memory: An Interdisciplinary Approach*, Oxford: Peter Lang.

Smith, Mark S.
   2004 *The Memoirs of God: History, Memory and the Experience of the Divine*, Minneapolis: Augsburg Fortress.

Chapter Seven

Knowledge, Judgment, Belief

History, as I have said before, is not a science, but an art—a narrative art—that involves a certain amount of scientific epistemology. As an intellectual discipline, the study of history is ostensibly judged not by aesthetic or moral values but by its claims to knowledge. As I argued in chapter 1, however, historical knowledge is of a certain, qualified kind. It is the nature and acquisition of this knowledge that forms the subject of this chapter.

Historical knowledge is critically attained, but is subject—like most forms of knowledge—to degrees of probability. In this it differs from the knowledge of cultural memory, which is not interested in critically acquired knowledge, but involves belief and commitment to a story. Historical knowledge is gained primarily by the interrogation of sources, and we can distinguish basically two procedures. One is to focus on what the evidence (typically a narrative) says and to consider whether what it relates can be considered a historical fact. The other is to focus on the nature of the source itself: where it comes from, who wrote it, and how well informed about the past it is likely to be.

It may be useful to preface the following discussion with a review of how Lester Grabbe, the most prolific historian of the present generation, advocates historical methodology. Grabbe is an extremely pragmatic practitioner, for whom the goal of the historian is to state what happened, what may have happened, and what may not have happened. In *Ancient Israel: What Do We Know and How Do We Know It?* (2007), he includes an introduction to aims and methods. Here he insists that primary sources should be preferred to secondary ones: primary sources stand at one remove from what they describe, while secondary sources depend on the primary ones. But he adds that while archaeology and inscriptions provide primary sources, "the biblical text is almost always a secondary source, written and edited long after the events ostensibly described" (35). Some modern biblical historians will quibble with that, and Grabbe recognizes that within the biblical text lie earlier sources, but that these have to be extracted in a fairly reliable way before they can rank with the other primary sources. Such a source might be the "book of the kings of Judah" (repeatedly cited in the books of Kings and Chronicles) or a critically reconstructed source like the "Court History of David." However, whether any of these sources are real; or if real, whether they are firsthand; or what they may have contained are all matters of conjecture. One quite fanciful example of a reconstructed source is Baruch Halpern's reconstruction of a stele erected by David (Halpern 2001, 195), the kind of speculation that makes so much of Halpern's work fascinating, but in the manner of historical fiction rather than history. Halpern is an excellent example of a historian who has no explicit or implicit method for using sources other than to conjure up as much detail as possible from any kind of clue: highly entertaining to read, but not a model for a historian to follow.

Grabbe divides the historian's approach into three steps: sources; analysis and synthesis, which we could paraphrase as identification; and understanding and interpreting. But rather than proposing any general procedures or assumptions, Grabbe believes that each episode or event has to be judged on its own merits, that all judgments are provisional and must be argued. Grabbe's many history books follow this procedure: a review of all relevant sources, a discussion, and then a reconstruction of what may have happened. In his 2007 volume, he concludes those chapters that deal most directly with the biblical narrative with four sections: "biblical data confirmed," "biblical data not confirmed, though they may be correct," "biblical picture incorrect," and "biblical picture omits/has gaps" (164–66; 212–15). In what follows I elaborate on what is fundamentally a fairly sound approach. The one respect in which I would add to his treatment, however, is that taking each case on its merits does not necessarily get us far and that we may need to consider more exhaustively the nature of the Bible as a whole and of its narratives. But I shall start with the (apparently) more straightforward issues.

Verification

We begin with the techniques of focusing on a narrated event (archaeological data will be considered presently). Such narrated events can fall into three categories: those that can be verified, those that can be disproved, and those that can be neither verified nor disproved (this scheme actually fits Grabbe's). The last category can only be dealt with by considering the nature of the sources and/or by applying various criteria of probability. The principle of verification relates to the highest degree of probability, and although some historians may concede that verification itself has degrees of probability, I prefer to use the term in a stricter sense, as applying to cases where we "know" that something is historical or not. The single principle here is independent attestation. If two independent accounts describe the same event, it is reasonable to conclude that the only basis for such an agreement is the event itself. This is the forensic equivalent of having two witnesses testify and having their testimony agree; we "know" the event occurred in the same way that the judge or the jury will "know" that a convicted person is guilty. In most cases the independent accounts will relate different versions of the event, but insofar as the details agree, we should conclude that they tell us something that really did happen (though how we describe or explain it is another matter).

Verification is possible in the case of broader historical phenomena. For example, we know that there was a kingdom referred to as "house of Omri," which can be identified with Israel; we know that circumcision was a mark of Jewish ethnicity in the Greco-Roman period, and we know any number of entities and circumstances that can be deduced from a multiplicity of sources, whether direct or indirect. Where we infer a *necessary* state of affairs, we are also verifying; but where we infer only a *possible* or even *probable* state of affairs, we are working within the domain of probability (discussed later).

We can also verify that something did *not* occur. Verifying a negative is more difficult than verifying a positive, and more commonly it is a matter of inference. Where sources contradict each other, we can know that at least one is not historically correct, but we cannot necessarily know which. The biblical narratives contain several contradictions, as illustrated in chapters 2 and 3. Most instances of possible negative verification (= disproof) involve archaeology, which will be treated separately.

In cases of conflict of evidence we can also construct a series of logical inferences such that if one item is false, another is true, or also false. For example, according to Ezra and Nehemiah, Bethel belonged, in the fifth century, to the territory of Judah, and the province consisted of the tribes of Judah, Benjamin, and Levi (or some of Levi?). So, according to Joshua 18:13, 22, Bethel lies in the territory of Benjamin. But according to the books of Kings, as well as Amos and Hosea, Bethel was a royal sanctuary of the kingdom of Israel during the Israelite monarchy, and according to Joshua 16 it belonged to Ephraim. There is a contradiction between two sets of data on each side, since Benjamin is said to have been part of Judah from the reign of Rehoboam (1 Kgs. 12). A number of inferences are possible from these statements. If Bethel belonged to Benjamin, then 1 Kings 12 is wrong and Benjamin was part of the kingdom of Israel. If Bethel was part of Ephraim, it was not included in the Assyrian province of Samaria and became part of Judah by the fifth century. Knowledge of one piece of information would in this case also provide knowledge of another.

This may seem irrelevant so long as we cannot know which are the correct statements, but it is important to recognize that we can say that *something* must be wrong. It might, for example, be claimed that none of the statements about Bethel can be disproved individually. But we could argue that nevertheless some of the information must be false, even if we do not know which.

The final comment on verification has to be that it is important in the sense that it provides the only reliable knowledge that we have. But it also has a drawback in that it can be applied only to a small number of cases. Most of the narratives in the Bible cannot be verified and have to be known as historical or not in a more qualified sense.

Correlating Literature and Archaeology

A special category of verification is constituted by archaeological data. A great deal of bad scholarship has been done by focusing on "one case at a time" and finding correlations between bits of text and archaeological data. I have already explained that biblical and archaeological data are so different in kind that using them in a process of verification (or falsification) is difficult. To illustrate some of the absurdities that can arise, here are some examples of convergences taken to indicate the historical reliability of the book of Judges, taken from a recent popular book (Dever 2001, 125):

> The metaphor of "tents"; "every man to his own tent." Gideon only has 300 men. These correlate to small, simple villages with populations of 100–300.

> Gideon called while plowing in his father's field; the Nazirite vow as rejection of urban values. These correlate to an agrarian economy and lifestyle, based partly on new agricultural technologies.

> The "shibboleth/sibboleth" story indicates local dialects; as yet no national language and script. This correlates to the few inscriptions in old Canaanite script, including an abecedary.

> A few inscriptions in old Canaanite script, including an abecedary; personal names that will appear in later Hebrew.

Most readers, however scanty their knowledge of the ancient world, will know that Palestine was agrarian and covered in small villages for the entire period covered by the Bible (including the New Testament), that literacy rates were always low, that the rejection of urban values is clearly reflected in the Gospels, that local dialects persisted as long as Hebrew was spoken (the Qumran scrolls provide eloquent evidence), and that personal names do not necessarily undergo any change over centuries. However, Dever balances these over-optimistic claims by commenting that "there can be none of what I have called 'nostalgia for a biblical past that never existed'" (2001, 62). He therefore believes that archaeology can disprove biblical narrative as clearly as it can prove it, and his recent works suggest that he believes archaeologists are best equipped to write the history of ancient Israel.

Whether archaeology alone provides adequate data for anything more than a fairly sketchy history of material culture in a given region is doubtful, but can it help to verify or disverify the biblical account to any useful degree? Finkelstein and Silberman (2001, 2006) have used a technique rather similar to excavating a tell, by stratifying aspects of the biblical narratives, identifying diagnostic features, and correlating these with what archaeology can reveal. They provide (2006, 26–30) a convenient summary of literary and archaeological features that are being matched, from "bandit tales" (David) and the chief of a tribal confederation (Saul) in the tenth century, through court ballads reflecting a developed monarchic state, to the portrait of a monarch in the imperial Assyrian style (Solomon) in the early seventh century and immediate reflections of Josiah's religious reforms (late seventh century).

The result is open to many kinds of query. One is that archaeology can document changes in culture that typically take effect over a century or more. Where greater precision is offered this is usually a biblical datum. Over fifty years ago Gerhard von Rad (1956) dated one of the pentateuchal sources, the Yahwist, to the "Solomonic enlightenment," and Finkelstein and Silberman seem to be creating a similar Josianic enlightenment. Like von Rad, however, their scholarly construct owes more to the Bible than to archaeology. Another query is why the authors nowhere consider the possibilities of literary composition beyond the Josianic era, even though not just Chronicles but also the final stages, at least, of Kings, belong to the neo-Babylonian or Persian (or even Hellenistic) era. Indeed, the neo-Babylonian period furnishes a very plausible setting for stories about Saul, if not for the beginnings of the Deuteronomistic History (see Edelman 2001, Davies 2007).

This technique is not one of verification. The archaeology has still been interpreted to *fit* the narratives and the narratives sectioned to correspond to the archaeology. It is an exercise of synthesis, always likely to involve a great deal of speculation and imagination. Methodologically it is undoubtedly a more sophisticated way to link the two kinds of data, and Finkelstein and Silberman's efforts explain the biblical narratives and the archaeology in a single thesis, and do not simply illustrate one by the other. Whether any closer integration can ever be achieved remains to be seen. In particular, whether the biblical texts can be stratified like a tell is debatable; many scholars do so, dividing either "vertically" with major sources undergoing periodic revisions, or "horizontally" with major blocks set side by side. But the composition of the narratives may be much more complex. There is also the challenge of those who argue that all the biblical texts are later than the monarchic era, in which case the rather unsatisfactory archaeology of this period needs to be brought into account too. But the composition of the biblical text is an issue unlikely to be resolved, and any attempt at a synthesis is reasonable if it can account for both the textual and the archaeological data.

Reliability

Like Finkelstein and Silberman, the historian should not always focus on the individual event, but consider also the nature of the sources themselves. A good deal of recent controversy about biblical history has revolved around the issue of the Bible's "reliability." Some participants in this controversy claim to defend the Bible's integrity or reliability or historicity against those who attack or impugn it. On the other side, there are those who have come to regard so much of it as fictional that they question whether it has any substantial reliability at all.

It should already be obvious to the reader of this book that "reliability" cannot be made into a matter of principle, but only of degree. The textual sources are of course all "reliable" in terms of their intended function, if we can discover what that is. Inscriptions are usually propagandistic and "reliably" convey the intended propaganda. The biblical sources, I have suggested, convey cultural memories, which have their own purposes in constructing identity and making sense of the present and the future. These memories can be relied on to reflect the view of the past that the authors wish to present. Artifacts cannot deliberately deceive, but the way in which they are recovered and interpreted is not innocent. Reliability in terms of historical facticity is another matter. Biblical narratives sometimes narrate what we modern historians believe to be historical facts, sometimes what we do not believe to be historical facts, and sometimes historical events or persons in what we believe to be a distorted way. There will be disagreement about some of these cases, but all such decisions rest on contradictions either within the biblical narratives or between them and other sources. The real problems arise in respect of the vast majority of narrated events, for which there is no other source. Did Abraham let Sarah join the royal harem in order to benefit himself; did David order Uriah's death; did Elijah say this or that to Ahab? There are no conceivable circumstances in which we would ever discover most of this. We are entitled—and we may even feel obliged—to make a judgment about whether these things are history or not.

Marc Brettler has discussed the evidential value of literary sources in relation to the ninth century BCE, though his treatment can easily be applied to other periods (Brettler 2007). He begins with the question of genre and suggests the following three questions be put to the text:

1. "Is this a text that is trying to recount the real past, or a text that is *not* trying to recount the real past?"
2. "If it is a text that *is* trying to recount the 'real past,' is it nevertheless useful for the modern historian trying to reconstruct the past?"

3. "If it is a text that *is* trying to recount the 'real past,' is it doing so in a reliable fashion?"

Brettler agrees that it is often difficult to identify the genre of an ancient text, so how can we know whether its authors are trying to recount a real past? As he points out, the stories of Genesis 1–11, of the patriarchs and of the later kings of Israel and Judah, cannot be distinguished from each generically. Many scholars presume that the biblical historians were indeed trying to recount the past. Brettler cites Halpern (1988) who claims an "antiquarian interest" on the part of the biblical historians, and Barton (2004, 104). He asks, nevertheless, whether such accounts are really using traditions about the past for other purposes. As he says, no ancient history is writing about the past without other purposes being present, and there is little interest in the real truth; in historical veracity; in premodern, including biblical, history. An interest in telling stories about the past is not necessarily an interest in the real past. That may seem an obvious point, but where the Bible is concerned it often seems to be overlooked.

Brettler does think, however, that there are certain markers that identify text as clearly *not* having an interest in the "real past." These include "didactic historical texts" such as Psalm 78, which seeks to demonstrate Judah's preeminence over the other tribes, or Psalms 78, 106, and 136, which is why these psalms depict the same historical events differently. There are also "symbolic historical texts," such as Ruth, Jonah, and Job (he might have mentioned Esther). This category would include what might be called parables or fables or allegories, whose meaning is metaphorical and not literal. Brettler notes that Ruth does have a marker of "real historical interest" in presenting Boaz as an ancestor of David, but we might ask ourselves whether this genealogy is not also to be taken symbolically (compare the genealogy of Jesus in Matthew, which is clearly symbolic). Even if such stories might also be literally true, the point is that this is not their main purpose, and so their meaning does not depend on the veracity of what has occurred. A similar mistake would be to look for the inn where the Good Samaritan left the victim (there is, of course a structure from a much later time that bears this title) or the pigsty at which the Prodigal Son worked.

Internal criteria for Brettler, then, achieve nothing: he rightly dismisses "verisimilitude" because, as everyone knows, this is characteristic of good historical fiction. That there is a country called Moab and a town called Bethlehem, that there are harvests and quaint customs of retaining land within families does not make the events in Ruth historical any more than ships or the port of Jaffa make Jonah a real tale—quite aside from fish inside which a man can fall and live for three days. In the end, then, Brettler resorts to external sources—in other words, verification.

Where the historian has exhausted the scope for verification, what is left? One option that Brettler does not explore here, though he has done so elsewhere (Brettler 1995), is an examination of the biblical sources as a whole to see what can be learned of their origin and purpose. Traditionally, critical biblical historians have used the range of textual, source, form, redaction, and tradition criticism to achieve this. More recently, other forms of literary analysis, such as ideological criticism, have also been used to locate the interests of the authors and the function of their writings. The use of these methods is well described in other books, and I do not discuss them here. Yet again, there are problems: one is scholarly disagreement about the authorship of the sources; another is possible doubt about the reliability of the critical methods; yet another the danger of circularity in locating the authors within a history of their own making.

Given these difficulties, it is tempting for the historian to cut the Gordian knot by making a judgment about general reliability or unreliability from what can be verified or disverified. Either of these can even be presumed, without any critical grounds, simply as a necessary step, on the grounds that if we have no biblical sources we have very little else. But such an uncritical move, I suggest, is an abdication of the historian's task. If we cannot generate historical knowledge of the past, we should not try to, and certainly not repeat stories. But if we apply some reasoning in formulating a judgment about general reliability, this procedure may be defensible.

A good deal of the current controversy in fact derives from these judgments (or presumptions), which I examine in more detail in the next chapter. Here I simply comment that verdicts of reliability or unreliability are morally equal. Those in favor of the reliability approach sometimes imply that belief and trust are virtuous, while doubt and mistrust are bad. Those who favor the unreliability approach sometimes accuse those of the opposite approach of being religiously motivated, which is not necessarily the case. Analogies can certainly be drawn for either approach. For example, it is a legal principle in most countries that an accused person is deemed innocent until or unless proven guilty. However, "historically unreliable" should not be equated with "guilty" unless one assumes that the biblical narratives are legally obliged to be historically accurate. The analogy of testimony is better, and in law a single uncorroborated testimony may be accepted (if on oath), though ironically enough biblical and Jewish law requires two witnesses, implying that a single witness should not be trusted. Further analogies are found in investigative and sensationalistic journalism. For the former, checking sources for corroboration is a matter of procedure, and doubting what one is being told (especially by politicians and public relations staff) is a standard attitude. By contrast, the sensationalistic press is generally unconcerned about these things and likes good stories.

When applied rigorously and consistently to the production of a modern narrative, the two options just reviewed produce two outcomes. One will be a history that almost certainly contains nonfacts, things we do not really know; not even *probably* know; the other will leave out things that might in fact be historical. A history written by a doubter will leave gaps of fact, explanation, and plot. In both aesthetic and practical terms it will be less than satisfactory. The history of a believer will be fuller in terms of what it includes as events and in terms of explanation, but it will be less trustworthy on its own account. Another aspect of the alternative is that the minimal history produced by the doubter is, ideally, open toward more history, toward discovering historical events previously discounted; that is the only direction in which it can progress. The maximal history of the believer progresses in the opposite direction, of discounting previously known facts. In this sense, one has a positive orientation despite its negative assumption, and the other a negative orientation despite its positive assumption.

A good case can be made for having both kinds of history available, and for readers to study both kinds, so that they become aware of the gap between what we probably know and what we might possibly know. We should, incidentally, also produce histories from different viewpoints so as to remind ourselves that every history is *someone's* history, reflecting particular values and allegiances and not others, and obliging us to recognize that no single history can ever be true.

Nevertheless, there is one condition to be laid before proponents of either option. I have insisted several times that the business of the modern biblical historian is to explain the biblical narratives as products of the past, of history. This means, for the doubting historian, explaining the purpose of what is being suspected as fiction. The believing historian apparently does not encounter so directly the challenge of explaining why a historical account should have been written: the answer is simply that these things happened. But in fact an explanation should still be demanded, because writing down what happened does not seem to have occurred to any other ancient human being as a natural response to events, except in a very limited and pragmatic way. So let us say that whether or not the historian is inclined to adopt a basically doubting or believing approach, it is necessary to explain the creation of the account itself, which in turn provides some rationale for an assessment of reliability.

These considerations apply, however, outside issues of verification and falsification. No historian who insists that the biblical narrative is either totally accurate or totally inaccurate as a historical source is to be trusted. There are historical facts contained in the narratives; there are also fictions. No presumption in favor of reliability or unreliability can override individual cases where we can reach a firm conclusion.

Probability

Assessment of probability is essential in the historian's task of converting narratives into history. As repeated many times, historical knowledge is *probable* knowledge; it is just that some facts belong to quite a different order of probability that constitute historical knowledge. The calculation of lesser orders of probability is in principle a scientific exercise, too, open to argument and reason and dispute. It is not an art. I pointed out in chapter 1 that while modern history writing is obliged to respect the principle of probability, it must be the case that improbable things happen. Therefore, historical reconstructions based on probability will at times be wrong, though we shall never know unless or until new data or arguments transfer them into the area of verified or disverified. But improbable events fall outside the competence of history to reconstruct, unless arguments can be found to make their occurrence probable. Perhaps nothing illustrates better than this example the limits of history and historical knowledge.

What factors may legitimately be brought into play when calculating probability? In recent years new dimensions have entered modern biblical history writing: the social sciences and the long-term environmental perspective of the French *Annales* school. The latter is in a sense extra-historical because it explicitly moves outside the domain of purely human affairs and considers the role of the physical environment. Such an analysis requires a long-term view of the past, in which large-scale patterns can be discerned. Study of climatic and ecological change, along with constants such as geography and landscape can reveal different, deeper, or broader systems of cause and effect that are imperceptible at the more microscopic level of years, decades, or even centuries, or the microcosmic arena of village, land state, or even empire. For this perspective, the term *longue durée* has been coined. Such a perspective can have an effect on the writing of biblical history, in that configurations typical of one period can be traced over longer periods of time. In the Middle Bronze Age (2000–1550 BCE) a system of city-states emerged in Palestine that declined in the Late Bronze (1550–1250 BCE). To judge from the evidence of the Amarna letters, which testify to that decline in the mid-fourteenth century, when Palestine was part of the Egyptian empire, the two prominent highland cities were Jerusalem and Shechem. The biblical stories as well as the archaeological data seem to point to a temporary disruption of that pattern. But the city-state system did not collapse totally: many cities continued and were absorbed into the new structures of territorial states represented by Aram, Ammon, Moab, Israel, and Judah. Shechem seems to have lost some prominence as a political center and Jerusalem perhaps recovered its dominance of Judah only in the eighth century. But in the Hellenistic period Shechem and Jerusalem were the religious centers within a Palestine that again belonged to an Egyptian empire under the Ptolemies. Does this suggest an underlying pattern, or is it a coincidence? Do immediate causes totally explain such configurations, or are there deeper factors that tend to reproduce them?

The social sciences have introduced several new techniques for the calculation of probability. The development of social anthropology has established an empirical basis for the study of how societies evolve, and from this basis a body of theory has emerged. For example, empirically based and theoretically informed analyses of state formation have enabled historians to consider in a stronger light the rise of Israel and Judah from isolated villages, extended families, tribes, and chiefdoms to kingdoms. The probabilities of these reconstructions can be gauged on the body of knowledge provided by anthropology. Similarly, the economic structures of agrarian, urban, and imperial systems can be examined in the light of a wealth of empirical data and theories derived from them. The strategies of imperial systems, ancient and modern, have also been examined, with fruitful results for the biblical historian examining the impact of Assyria and its successors. To a lesser extent, recent developments in literary and ideological criticism, especially those influenced by Marxist analysis, have brought language and literature into the domain of historical study, recognizing literary texts as sites of political and social contestation, or as creating structures of thought that influence or even dominate the worldview of societies. (We might add, creating cultural memories.) The effect of all these factors on the assessment of probability is considerable, and they permit us to create modern historical narratives without lapsing into agnosticism or uncritical reproduction of sources whose reliability we simply do not know.

The adoption of these methods in biblical studies is part of the process by which it is being assimilated into general historical discourse and the ancient histories of Israel and Judah integrated into the universal human past. Like the natural sciences, the social sciences develop laws about human behavior, but unlike the hard sciences these laws cannot be empirically tested in a laboratory. In any case, they do not have the status of rules that can deliver scientific knowledge about the past or predict individual outcomes. The "law of averages" is a good example of the kind of knowledge that can be obtained. They do not enable anyone to predict the next toss of a coin, or any toss of any coin. Likewise, the probable behavior of large numbers of people can be predicted, whereas individual behavior is much less predictable, if predictable at all. Now, many historians believe that history is to a large extent the behavior of individuals and occurrences of single, unique events, which cannot be properly explained by any kind of social-scientific "law." In other words, it is essentially a humanistic discipline that seeks to find out what happened in individual cases determined by unpredictable human behavior. I do not propose to enter that debate here but only to comment that such a humanistic approach to biblical history would have little prospect of generating any new historical understanding or knowledge; it has no resources for doing much beyond glossing the biblical story. Unless the biblical historian decides to ignore archaeology, whose deductions rely a great deal on social-scientific "laws," these sorts of calculations are in any case already being made.

Biblical historians have regularly tried another method of establishing the probability of an event. Analysis of the history of biblical texts can lead to a reconstruction of the growth of the content. Tradition history is the subdiscipline that redefines such a history. One premise of this deduction (not strictly a necessary one, but nevertheless hard to avoid), is that the earlier stages of the tradition bring us close to the reality of the event being recollected. In a strict sense this is true, of course: the earlier the stage of the tradition, the closer we are chronologically to the event. The assumption that therefore the older the tradition the more reliable it is also probably strikes most people as commonsensical. But this assumption can be tested, and the results show that it does not necessarily follow.

An analysis undertaken by Axel Knauf (2008) on the first part of the book of Joshua illustrates how earlier does not necessarily mean more accurate. Knauf sets out the following literary history of Joshua: it is of course only one of several theories, but the test can be applied using others (asterisks indicate earlier forms of the present biblical text).

Late seventh century	First draft, end of an Exodus–Conquest–Story (Josh. 6* and 10*)
525–450	Exodus–Conquest–Story incorporated into Deuteronomistic History (Josh. 6–11*)
450–400	First Hexateuch Redaction (Josh. 1–11*; 15:20–18:1*)
400–375	Second Hexateuch Redaction (Josh. 13; 20–22; 24) Joshua–Judges–Redaction (Josh. 12; 14; 18–19; 23)

Then he provides a list of cities and where we have the evidence, when they existed.

The ratios at the bottom show how often the text at its various junctures accurately names existing cities. The ratios at the bottom do not show decreasing accuracy as time progresses: indeed, the earliest layer (on Knauf's dating) is the least accurate. Obviously further analyses of this kind are needed, to see whether similar results can be obtained. But at least the one exercise that has been carried out warns us not to make assumptions about the increasing reliability of data as we go further back; we must remember that cultural memory is more complex than this and does not correspond to a unlinear tradition.

City	Exod–Josh* (seventh century)	Deut History (525–450)	1 Hexateuch (450–400)	2 Hexateuch (400–375)	Josh–Judg (400–375)
Jericho	×	×	×	×	×
Ai	—	×	×	×	×
Jerusalem	✔	✔	✔	✔	✔
Hebron	×	✔	✔	✔	✔
Yarmut	×	×	×	×	×
Lachish	✔	✔	✔	✔	✔
Eglon	×	×	×	×	×
Makedah	—	×	×	×	×
Libna	—	×	×	×	×
Gezer	—	✔	✔	✔	✔
Debir	—	×	×	×	×
Hazor	—	✔	✔	✔	✔
Madon	—	×	×	×	×
Shimron	—	✔	✔	✔	✔
Akshaf	—	✔	✔	✔	✔
Heshbon	—	—	—	×	×
Bashan	—	—	—	×	×
Geder	—	—	—	—	×
Horma	—	—	—	—	×
Arad	—	—	—	—	×
Adullam	—	—	—	—	×
Bethel	—	—	—	—	×
Tappuah	—	—	—	—	×
Hefer	—	—	—	—	×
Afek	—	—	—	—	✔
Taanach	—	—	—	—	✔
Megiddo	—	—	—	—	✔
Kedesh	—	—	—	—	×
Jokneam	—	—	—	—	✔
Dor	—	—	—	—	✔
Gilgal	—	—	—	—	×
Tirzah	—	—	—	—	×
ratio	2/6	7/15	7/15	7/17	12/32
	0.33	0.47	0.47	0.41	0.38

Belief

A final, special issue relating to probability is the miraculous. This principle applies not only or even especially to the Bible; most ancient histories include miraculous events, just as most modern novels include chance and coincidence. If we choose to include miracles, then we shall end up not writing history, for two reasons. First, "miracle" is not a category of *event*, but a category of *interpretation of an event* that ascribes divine causality to something that seems to have no rational explanation. In the same category is spirit possession, which is not a fact but an interpretation of a mental or physical disorder which biblical narratives adopt, and which reflect the common cultural knowledge of the times. Second, the discipline of history is based on rational explanation. If historians allow each other to claim that such-and-such an event was caused by divine (or extraterrestrial) intervention, we are allowing a cause that cannot be verified not just empirically but metaphysically, and, more importantly, cannot be controlled. What if all history is really dictated by supernatural beings? That was a widespread belief in ancient societies, including, probably, ancient Israel and Judah. If that is the case, then history is a waste of time: we can neither understand nor explain it. Human motivation is irrelevant, since it is all in principle due to supernatural direction.

In my view, modern history writing, by its very nature, cannot include miraculous explanation, even if the historian as an individual may believe in such things. It can be regarded, after all, as a subspecies of improbable event of the kind that the historian is not allowed to propose. Whether miracles happen, like whether earth has been invaded in the past by extraterrestrials, is something that lies outside the competence of history to explain.

"What Did the Biblical Writers Know?"

This phrase forms part of the title of a recent book by William Dever (though Dever does not answer the question), and echoed by Grabbe (2007). If we add to it, "What *could* the biblical writers know?" we have formulated the two basic questions that the modern historian needs to ask. Ancient writing about the past is dictated by two considerations: what has been told before and what needs to be told now. What has been told before can include any sort of information about the past, comprising cultural memories of various social groups—villages, scribes, traders, families, priests. The second consideration provides the motivation for writing another story—or perhaps, even for writing a story at all in the first place. The story needs retelling, and not in the way that oral recitation varies, but something a little less transient, not immediately lost, and something to be shared. So what writers put down is not quite what they receive. We cannot assume, either, that what the writers received or what they pass on were things that actually occurred, or that the writers knew whether or not they had occurred. Concern with such questions is our modern problem, and exists only in a culture that can research the past, developing a notion of history as "what really happened." We cannot in the end pass on this responsibility to ancient authors who had no such problem and berate them for not being reliable enough for our purposes. Instead, we must do the best we can to find out what the ancient authors did not know, and did not seem to care about knowing.

Summary

The basic tools and procedures that the modern historian can use are fairly well agreed upon, and while a range of approaches is possible, they are all well known and widely accepted. Much of the time, the modern biblical historian is unable to produce "historical knowledge." So much of what the biblical narratives cover, and what the archaeological and epigraphic remains attest, is irretrievable. Most often we can only state whether in our opinion something is likely, possible, or probable to have occurred. These judgments are not (or should not be) arbitrary and need not be too much influenced by ideological preferences. There remain various options and scope for disagreements. There is, or should be, common ground in the art of writing history and the science of assembling evidence and argument.

I have moved more or less systematically from cases where we can verify and falsify, to those where we can only express probability, and examined the issues that control judgments. But I have been concerned with how the historian might work rather than what concrete historical conclusions might be reached.

References

Barton, John
    2004 "Dating the Succession Narrative," in J. Day (ed.), *In Search of Pre-Exilic Israel*, London: T&T Clark, 95–106.

Brettler, Marc Zvi
    1995 *The Creation of History in Ancient Israel*, London: Routledge.
    2007 "Method in the Application of Biblical Source Material to Historical Writing (with Particular Reference to the Ninth Century BCE)," in H. G. M. Williamson (ed.), *Understanding the History of Ancient Israel*, Oxford: Oxford University Press, 305–36.

Davies, Philip R.
    2007 *The Origins of Biblical Israel*, London: T&T Clark.

Dever, William G.
    2001 *What Did the Biblical Writers Know and When Did They Know It? What Archaeology Can Tell Us about the Reality of Ancient Israel*, Grand Rapids: Eerdmans.

Edelman, Diana
    2001 "Did Saulide-Davidic Rivalry Resurface in Early Persian Yehud?" in M. P. Graham and A. Dearman (eds.), *The Land That I Will Show You: Essays in the History and Archaeology of the Ancient Near East in Honor of J. Maxwell Miller*, Sheffield: Sheffield Academic Press, 70–92.

Finkelstein, Israel, and Neil Asher Silberman
    2001 *The Bible Unearthed: Archaeology's New Vision of Ancient Israel and the Origin of Its Sacred Texts*, New York: Free Press.
    2006 *David and Solomon: In Search of the Bible's Sacred Kings and the Roots of the Western Tradition*, New York: Free Press.

Grabbe, Lester L.
    2007 *Ancient Israel: What Do We Know and How Do We Know It?* London: T&T Clark.

Halpern, Baruch
    1988 *The First Historians: The Hebrew Bible and History*, New York: Harper and Row.

    2001 *David's Secret Demons: Murderer, Messiah, Traitor, King*, Grand Rapids: Eerdmans.

Knauf, E. Axel
    2008 "History in Joshua," Paper read at the 2008 meeting of the European Association of Biblical Studies, Vienna.

von Rad, Gerhard
    1961 *Genesis*, Old Testament Library, Philadelphia: Westminster Press.

Chapter Eight

A Tale of Two Histories

It is now time to do a kind of history of histories, which is only slightly less problematic than a biblical history. In fact, I admit from the outset that this is no history but a set of reflections on some recent and contemporary efforts and their outcomes. But before embarking on this—and to help put it in context—let me summarize the main points I have made in this book.

1. Doing history with the Bible requires us to understand how its narratives about the past work.
2. The Bible itself is a historical datum, and any modern history of ancient Israel and Judah must include an explanation of what it is and how, when, and why it came into being.
3. "Cultural memory" is a better description than "history" or "tradition" for the stories we have in the Bible, both in their character and their function.
4. There are no special methods, techniques, or issues involved in doing biblical history. The Bible is a unique source in many ways, but not beyond comparison with other ancient literatures. (Classical historians work with even more extensive and varied literary resources.) The basic tools and procedures that the modern historian uses are fairly well agreed; they can and should be applied.

5. Even when using standard tools and procedures, even the same data, different outcomes are possible. There is no single authoritative or objectively correct account of the past, because the past that we write about is really only those relics that happen to have survived, not a reliable indication of the totality of past events. And we ourselves are the true authors of history; without our narratives, it does not exist.

From these points two conclusions important for this chapter emerge. One is that there are good and bad histories: those that use the data and tools properly and those that don't (or do not use *any* tools!). But there can be more than one good history. We should not tolerate bad history, even if we rather like what we hear, but we should embrace a variety of good histories, because multi-dimensional perspectives improve our understanding not only of the past but also of the present. Sharing our different histories is an important aid to negotiating our (often conflicting) cultural memories. And since the biblical narratives still function widely as a (canonized) cultural memory, good biblical history can and should play an important moderating role in such negotiations—though controversy is likely to arise.

The different poles of trust and doubt (or credulity and skepticism) that I discussed in the last chapter have come to be referred to in the last couple of decades as maximalism and minimalism. Current debate about biblical history is dominated by these two terms. They are sometimes used to refer to schools, but they are more like options, representing two different ways of tackling biblical history, usually (but not always) with the same tools. What is more, each of them tends to adopt its own history of biblical history writing. The term "revisionist" is frequently used of the minimalist option, though it has equally well been argued that the minimalist option is in fact the more traditional and reverses almost a century of conservative revisionism. There is perhaps no better illustration of using the past to justify the present.

The differences between the two options rest on two possible starting points for an assessment of the relationship between the biblical narratives of the past and the real past. One of these is external data: archaeology and ancient inscriptions. Until a few decades ago, these clues were not just interpreted, but sought as confirmation of the soundness of the biblical narratives. They were not evidence of something being argued but proof of something already accepted. But from the mid-twentieth century and especially since the 1970s, new archaeological data and their interpretation have been taken by proponents on the minimalist option as directly contradicting a large and important part of the biblical narrative—the sections that describe Israel's origins.

The other starting point is the origin of the biblical narratives. The maximalist option adheres to a monarchic date for most of the materials, though it accepts postmonarchic editing. The minimalist option tends to assign later dates. The dating, however, is not the real issue, but whether or not the stories have any direct link to the events they describe. For the maximalists they are largely reliable because they come from the same period as the events, or not too long afterward; for minimalists they are cut off from the events and so are imagining and creating a past whose contours are determined by the present context and a not-reliable recollection of the past—regardless of the historical data they undoubtedly contain in places.

The minimalist option arrived as an alternative agenda only recently, and its arrival gave birth to maximalism as a conscious option rather than, as its practitioners saw it, the simple default. A maximalist approach had been, mainly in Israel and the United States, the received wisdom for some time, but had not been defended as an approach because there was no systematic challenge. Rather, archaeology was (ab)used to demonstrate the historical validity of individual cases, without the basis for such comparison being carefully considered. In Europe, however, and especially in Germany and Italy, minimalist options have long been present. Before offering a short narrative of the two options, I shall try and explain how each of them is logically constructed.

The Minimalist Option

The minimalist option starts, typically, from recent archaeological data that have been interpreted by the great majority of archaeologists as configuring the origins of Israel in terms quite different from those in the Bible. As a result, the invention of a great deal of that narrative has to be taken seriously, in the sense of being provided with an explanation. The unreliability of such a large part of the narrative also encourages a very cautious attitude toward the remainder, with the view that nothing unverified can be assumed to have occurred.

Those following the minimalist option prefer later dates for the composition of the pentateuchal narrative and indeed other biblical literature because later dates provide better contexts for the creation of the stories. This is not just because of the gap in time that would be necessary to explain discrepancies between archaeological and biblical portraits of the past, but because later dates afford better political, social, and religious contexts for the enterprise. The later proposed dates range from the reign of Josiah (late seventh century, shortly before the end of the Judahite monarchy) to the Hellenistic period, with the Persian period figuring prominently. But how are these contexts determined? The answer is, by looking at ideology. The ideology of the texts does not lie all on the surface but also within and beneath the text. The concept itself and the tools for analyzing it have long been available from Marxist analysis and applied in other historical work, but there are other considerations. Most of the biblical literature is agreed by all biblical scholars to have reached its final shape after the end of the Judahite monarchy: this can support the minimalist option because if literary editing was obviously taking place, then the resources and motives for authoring texts can also have been present. Whether such writing and rewriting took place earlier remains, by contrast, conjectural.

Late dating is not, of course, automatically entailed in a minimalist view. Stories can in theory be early and unreliable, but also late and reliable. The real issue is the connection between the postulated events and the accounts: whether there is a gap between events and story. If the stories are essentially fictional, there is a gap. But if they were understood as elaborations or exaggerations of events that really occurred, then "fiction" would be an inaccurate term, and we might instead call them "tradition." If we regard

them as tradition, we would classify them as secondhand historical sources. The minimalist option starts from the judgment that
the origin story (from Genesis to Joshua or even later) cannot be
classified strictly as a tradition. It cannot, in other words, be traced
back through any continuous process, because there are no original events to which most of it corresponds and which would have
generated that tradition. A minimalist option is legitimate also for
the so-called united monarchy, which archaeological data are also
challenging. As for the time of the two kingdoms, the evidence of
inscriptions means that some historical correspondence must
obviously be allowed. But this does not necessarily validate the
reliability of the account, given the discrepancies in details and in
the evidence of artificial chronology, and problems in the portraits
of Hezekiah and Josiah; in short, anything that cannot be verified
in this period is also entitled to be doubted.

Cultural memory as a description of the contents of the biblical narratives suits the minimalist option quite well, because its
function is not to record the past but to appropriate it as a means
of creating and sustaining identity. Hence the origin of such stories is sought in a context where crises of identity may be found.

The Maximalist Option

The maximalist option has developed in two basic forms. One
adopts the same archaeological starting point as the minimalist
option but draws the opposite conclusion, denying that there is
any contradiction. This is a minority view: more common is the
claim that archaeological data are unreliable, being partial and
open to various interpretations. It is sometimes even suggested
that archaeology cannot really contradict a biblical account. (This
claim should mean, of course, that archaeology cannot *confirm* the
biblical account either.) The evidence of inscriptions also figures
prominently, as proof that kings of Israel and Judah really did live
and confront Assyria and Babylon. Hence, there are reasons to
accept that at least the books of Samuel–Kings retain historical
information and so rely on contemporary or informed sources.
The composition of much of the biblical literature is therefore

placed in the monarchic era, and this date in turn heightens the possible reliability of all the material. Inaccurate elements are explained, typically, as the outcome of a process of tradition; exaggeration and embellishment are often accepted, but the vital link between tradition and historical core is usually maintained.

While I believe that it is helpful to explain the current situation in terms of two options, it is not necessary for any historian to follow only one. As I have already pointed out, it is possible to make a different judgment about external evidence in the case of Kings and the Pentateuch. Future archaeological data may also affect how the books of Samuel, for example, are judged. Thus, one can take both options for different bits of biblical literature, and many historians, such as Miller and Hayes (1986, 2006) and Grabbe (2007) do just that. If nothing else, such choices are a reminder that the Bible is not a single source but a collection of sources that can be assessed differently.

Biblical History in Recent Debate

Now that I have explained both options in terms of the logic of their positions, we can offer another, more narrative kind of explanation (a fuller account of major developments can be found in Banks 2006), together with the kinds of histories these options produced. The seeds of the two options can be found already in the nineteenth-century debates over biblical criticism. It developed in the twentieth century as a conflict between humanistic and scientific models, but the opposition between a conservative/ evangelical context and a liberal theological/secular one was also very lively in the late nineteenth century. But while theological issues clearly underlay (and still do) much of the debate, doctrinal principles are rarely invoked as arguments. Before the midpoint of the twentieth century, Albrecht Alt and W. F. Albright and their followers were already applying the results of archaeology differently, principally with regard to the historicity of the patriarchs and of the conquest. The differences are best seen in comparing the *Histories* of Martin Noth and John Bright (the latter in the early editions). There was a corresponding difference in understanding the biblical narrative: the German tradition (we can also include here Gerhard von Rad) saw the biblical stories as Israel's traditions; the Albright school saw them rather more simply as witnesses to events. Hence Noth and von Rad were interested in tradition-history, how the biblical stories were assembled; for the Albright school, this was incidental: the stories were "recitals" of divine acts, a thesis directly expounded by G. Ernest Wright (1952).

However, despite strong disagreement over patriarchs and conquest, there was little dispute between Germany and the United States over the biblical narrative following the emergence/arrival of Israelites in Canaan. Neither Noth nor Bright abandoned the biblical storyline in any essential detail in their influential *Histories* (Bright 1959, Noth 1958). Noth proposed (and Bright agreed) that the nation had comprised a twelve-tribe "league" when it settled in Palestine, though for Noth this was the beginning of its history. The patriarchal stories were definitively questioned outside Germany by Thomas Thompson and John Van Seters in 1974 and 1975, respectively. But here too there was a significant divergence: Van Seters proposed an exilic date for the Abraham stories; Thompson did not believe they bore any relation to any particular period. The subsequent work of both scholars has followed the same line: Van Seters has dated a great deal of the Pentateuch to the exilic period, while Thompson has been increasingly convinced that the biblical narrative does not offer clues to a particular historical context.

Norman Gottwald's *Tribes of Yahweh* (1979) built on George Mendenhall's (1973) theory of Israel as Canaanites in revolution (thus contradicting the contents of Genesis–Joshua) but met with less initial agreement. By this time, as I narrated earlier, the West Bank survey of the 1970s had indicated that the population later to comprise much of Israel and Judah was local and had settled as farmers in the highlands, thus confirming Alt's hypothesis of nearly half a century earlier. In 1988 Niels Peter Lemche's *Ancient Israel* contained a chapter on text and history (29–73) stating that the biblical text was written later than the period it was supposedly describing, was secondary as a source, betrayed numerous revisions, and lacked independent verification. In his 1985 *Early*

Israel he argued that the history of ancient Israel cannot be derived directly from the Bible itself: the basis of critical evaluation lies in the "epigraphical, archaeological and regional history of *Palestine*" (his italics, 116–17). This is a clear statement of the minimalist option; later Lemche famously suggested that the Hebrew Bible is a "Hellenistic book" (Lemche, 2001).

The *Histories* of Miller and Hayes (1986), Ahlström (1993), and Soggin (1985) were more cautious, reflecting unease about converting Genesis–Joshua into history, but more accepting of Samuel and Kings. They therefore take different options for different parts of the Bible. The Semitic philologist Giovanni Garbini wrote on various themes relating to the Bible (collected in an English translation in 1988), displaying an independent and vigorously skeptical attitude toward the historicity of most of the biblical narrative, and although his suggestions are sometimes quixotic, Garbini influenced both Soggin and Lemche.

Noth's view of a tribal league, based on a Greek analogy, was demolished by de Geus (1976) and Lemche (1977 [based on a 1972 study in Danish]). This did not lead immediately to a rejection of the history of the book of Judges, but it did open again the question of how Israel actually came into being. Indeed, if Israel did originate in Palestine, could it have had any memories of having been in Egypt, in the wilderness, of having conquered the land from outside? Should we be speaking, as had Noth and most subsequent scholarship, of pentateuchal traditions?

Thomas Thompson's history of 1992 was an extensive presentation of the archaeological data and the source-critical theories of the Pentateuch, resulting in a very negative evaluation of the biblical narrative as a basis for historical reconstruction. His *The Bible in History/The Mythic Past* (1999) makes a detailed case for considering that the biblical texts nowhere deal with history at all and that nothing in the biblical narratives can be verified as a historical datum. It is true that the writers of these narratives do not, and do not try to, produce history in the way we do, but that they construct a past entirely in a metaphorical or allegorical way is not the view of most who follow the minimalist option. This, at any rate, is not exactly how cultural memory works.

My own *In Search of Ancient Israel* (1992) agreed with Thompson except in suggesting that a real historical context *could* be sought for the stories that created the biblical Israel. This short book was written as an attempt to pursue the implications of the research just mentioned, and addressed the question of how and why the biblical texts were produced. Arguing that the monarchic era offered no realistic context, either in terms of material culture or ideological requirement, I argued that "biblical Israel" was a retrojection into the past, part of an identity-building agenda by the elite of Judah in the Persian era. I did not suggest that there had been no Israel or Judah or that the texts were totally without historical data, nor did I then use the concept of cultural memory; but I would have argued that while some of the memories had a basis in recollection, others did not, and the canonized, national story created from the amalgamation of various memories was not historical.

I have since elaborated and modified that view, dissecting the various biblical Israels and proposing that the core of Judean writing about the past arises from the traumas of Jerusalem's destruction as capital and chief sanctuary, its replacement by the Benjaminite Mizpah and Bethel, and the reinstatement of Jerusalem at the end of the fifth century (2007). In 1992 I wished mainly to stress that the "ancient Israel" that modern historians referred to was an amalgam of an idealized, unhistorical, biblical society and a real ancient society that left relics for the archaeologist. Attributing the latter to the former was a complete mistake. My 2007 book argues that the biblical Israels show an attempt to create an Israelite nation that, unlike the Israelite kingdom centered on Samaria, did not historically exist.

At this point, the entire biblical historical narrative, not just the stories of Israel's early history, had come under review, and the figures of David and Solomon in particular were now in the front line. The surveys that "discovered" the original (proto-) Israel also suggested that the northern ("Ephraimite") highlands always led the southern (Judean) highlands in social, economic, and political development, and that what became the kingdom of Judah developed later than its northern neighbor. If we also bear in mind that no king before Omri is attested by epigraphic sources, the united monarchy remains unconfirmed (or unsupported). At the time of writing, the historical existence of David is the focus of very heated controversy, and no immediate resolution seems in sight, but it cannot easily be claimed as a piece of historical *knowledge*.

A couple of other important contributions should be mentioned. In 1995 Marc Brettler published a study entitled *The Creation of History in Ancient Israel*, in which he carefully demonstrated the range of techniques by which biblical writers dealt with the past, including typology, reinterpretation, and satire. If the concrete outcomes were not particularly dramatic, Brettler's work supports the minimalist contention that biblical narratives about the past do not translate easily into our modern category of history.

Keith Whitelam's *The Invention of Ancient Israel* (1996) added a new dimension to the debate and underlined its contemporary resonance by arguing that the history of ancient Palestine had been ignored and silenced by biblical studies because its object of interest has been an ancient Israel conceived and presented as the taproot of Western civilization. The book demonstrated, by means of extensive quotations, just how the image of biblical Israel (understood as "ancient Israel") was rooted in the West's own identity. Whitelam also pointed out—again, this is a matter of documented fact—that the history of ancient Palestine had been left to biblical historians, whose work was dominated by Israel and by the Bible (Ahlström being a partial exception). Whitelam's critique of the biblical sources and his earlier work, with Coote, on Israelite origins (Coote and Whitelam, 1987) led him to speak of the biblical Israel, and its modern scholarly counterpart, ancient Israel, as an "invention." In focusing on the contemporary relevance of the debate about history, Whitelam has highlighted how the Bible's history is not just an ancient Judean cultural memory but a modern Jewish, Christian, and Muslim one: all, for example, venerate Abraham as an ancestor, honor a line of divinely sent prophets, and view Jerusalem as a holy city.

The works just mentioned have set a framework, a set of questions and proposals, rather than a single thesis, and a large number of scholars are now working within that framework. None of these should be called "followers" (and *certainly* not members of a school!), for minimalism was not the invention of a small group—and certainly not a cohesive group—of scholars. Nor was minimalism an ideology. It was a response to the tensions between archaeology and biblical text, to developments within historical-critical studies, such as a greater emphasis on the roles of redactors as the real authors compared with their postulated sources, and the contribution of new literary criticism to issues of story, point of view, and ideology. It also recognized the loss of authorial (and *readerly*) innocence in the generating of textual meaning. It is therefore important to understand that the minimalist approach to biblical history writing is embedded in a broad range of issues and intellectual movements. Attacks on some of these scholars, including charges of anti-Semitism, incompetence, and undermining Western civilization, make little impact on the targets themselves but draw attention rather to the sometime unspoken but often obvious agendas of those making the charge.

Before turning to maximalist responses, let me summarize the thesis of the minimalist options. Archaeology and epigraphy are taken as the primary sources and the biblical sources as secondary. The biblical narrative is in fact in large part not even a secondary source for what it describes, but a construction, and as such is much more evidence of the social context that generated it. As a result, all biblical statements need some kind of support or verification before they can be considered as historical. But, given that the overlap between archaeology and epigraphy and the biblical data is relatively slight in both its content and in the kind of evidence of the past it offers, a great deal of the biblical narrative is unverifiable. So the fullest use of other methods, especially social-scientific techniques, is made to help in assessing probability. The date, setting, and purpose of the narratives are also examined as closely as the evidence permits, both to assess the possibility that these narratives have reliable information and to set their production into the history of the society that enabled or required it.

The recent book on biblical history by Moore (2006) provides a fuller and rather more nuanced analysis of the background from which the minimalist option emerged. Her treatment of what I call the two options, however, is quite different: she differentiates a distinct group of minimalists (Thompson, Lemche, Davies, Whitelam) from the remainder, whom she calls "non-minimalists" and in so doing I think overemphasizes the agreement between the minimalists and between her large body of non-minimalists. She also suggests that minimalists do not believe that history can be extracted from biblical texts, which is true only of Thompson. This perception is symptomatic, I suspect, of a view of scholarship from North America, where the minimal option is not widely explored, though it is far from absent. By contrast, European scholarship recognizes no consensus at all, and the minimalist option is expressed in a variety of opinions. The absence of a large quasi-scholarly conservative constituency obsessed with validating biblical historicity and a strong, especially German tradition of literary-historical analysis (with a correspondingly deeper knowledge of the biblical text itself) enables European scholars to explore rather more freely the intricate issues that the biblical texts generate. Of course, North American readers may feel differently, but I cannot see that maximalism is a default option; it is as much a clear methodological strategy as its alternative, and it also needs to be spelled out and defended.

The Maximalist Thesis

Only recently have explicitly maximalist histories or methodological essays been written, and these inevitably address the challenge of the minimalist option. I review here three recent books that represent what can be characterized as engagement, disengagement, and confrontation with that option, respectively that (a) the minimalist option is a possibility but does not prove that maximalism is not also a valid alternative; (b) the use of archaeology, any form of social-scientific research, and historical-critical scholarship are all invalid means of historical knowledge; and (c) archaeological data and inscriptions show that the Bible is mostly or totally reliable.

Jens Bruun Kofoed

Kofoed's book *Text History: Historiography and the Study of the Biblical Text* (2005) is mainly concerned to counter what he sees as the extreme skepticism of his Danish colleagues Thompson and Lemche. Kofoed argues that social-scientific approaches tend to exclude individual choices and improbabilities that texts record and thus imperfectly represent the human past. He does not put it as directly, but he is making the point (see chap. 5) that probabilities, on which the social sciences greatly rely for their interpretation, do not always occur. But why should we accept the detail that the texts provide? How can we determine that a particular event did in fact occur? While the minimalist option prefers to assume it did not occur unless we have a reason to think it did, Kofoed insists it is just as reasonable to say we assume it did unless we have reason to assume it did not, and in his defense he appeals to a number of factors that support a higher degree of reliability for the biblical narratives.

He starts with the dating of the narratives, considering the antiquity of the textual tradition and possible original sources, arguing (as does Nicholson 2004) that a lengthy period of time is presupposed by their literary history. He moves further back to the possibility of oral tradition underlying the biblical text and that this may preserve historical data. Further evidence of antiquity is furnished by arguing for the exclusively monarchic date of standard biblical Hebrew. He does not observe that some of the Qumran scrolls betray multiple textual editions of scriptural writings and recensions of sectarian documents that must have occurred over a short period, while the linguistic dating of biblical texts is currently being challenged (Young, Rezetko, and Ehrensvard, 2008). Finally, Kofoed asserts that texts can betray a historical consciousness and intent of their authors.

Kofoed accepts that he has only established possibilities. Are these possibilities as well established as the minimalist ones? Do they support the option of assuming the historicity of a text rather than the opposite? His arguments oblige him to accept literary-historical arguments but minimize the evidential value of archaeology. Yet in the end he recognizes the validity of the minimalist option while insisting that a maximalist one is also reasonable. As I understand his conclusion, he accepts that only further research will (or might) clarify which of the options is preferable. In this he is rather unusual among recent defenders of the maximalist option, who mostly seek to establish (like the two examples following) that the minimalist option is not valid—and, to be fair, unlike many who advocate the minimalist option, for whom a maximalist one is also no longer valid. But he does not, as several scholars do, suggest that each option is preferable for different biblical narratives.

Iain Provan, V. Phillips Long, and Tremper Longman
A Biblical History of Israel (2003) is not so easy to review because it contains an introductory section on methods and hermeneutics by Provan, followed by a co-written history proper, and the two parts seem in places to be contradictory. I focus here, therefore, on the introduction but occasionally point out where the execution seems to suggest otherwise.

Provan opens by attacking Keith Whitelam's claim to archaeological knowledge regarding the origins of Israel. He objects to Whitelam (who in this respect is representative of many who prefer a minimalist option) enhancing the role of archaeology and demeaning the biblical narrative by stating that archaeology "demonstrates" the fictionality of the biblical account when it seems to contradict, but "minimizing" the points of agreement. Provan takes the view, as I understand him, that archaeology does not provide any knowledge of the kind that justifies such a conclusion, and, I would infer, takes the view that it therefore cannot contradict the biblical narratives, in which case it obviously cannot confirm them either. It is irrelevant to the issue of their historicity.

I draw this inference from further remarks that Provan makes about the social sciences, but in discussing the conquest stories of the first half of the book of Joshua, the three authors conclude that "such archaeological evidence as is known to us in no way invalidates the biblical testimony" (192), suggesting that they do regard archaeological data as possibly relevant, and in principle capable of invalidating. They claim in fact that the interpretation of the data may be wrong, citing a minority of scholars who have challenged the almost unanimous finding that Jericho was not destroyed at the beginning of the Iron Age. The authors' view may therefore be that archaeology can, in principle, provide knowledge, but only when there is no disagreement over the interpretation of the data. But since there can always be at least one person to disagree, the outcome, in practice, is that archaeology is not considered valid evidence. (Since few scholarly conclusions are absolutely unanimous, this is actually a principle that, if extended generally, makes scholarship itself useless, and the same can be said of a good deal of science.)

The other main criticism that Provan has of Whitelam is his use of "ideology." The word can be used in both a neutral and a pejorative sense, and it seems that Provan, like Barr (2000), who gives general support to Provan's stance while offering extensive detailed criticisms, understands it negatively—and apparently considers that Whitelam does too. The danger of a negative definition—whoever uses it—is obvious, since its use can then be prejudicial: a Marxist might allow only a capitalist to have ideology and a capitalist only a Marxist to do so. It is foolish to claim that your opponents have ideology, but you do not. I personally find attacks on ideology as such, from any quarter, to be pointless. (Theology, for example, is clearly a certain kind of religious ideology.) Provan's insistence that evidence should take precedence over ideology (8) in making historical judgments nevertheless seems sensible. Yet while material artifacts do not usually possess an intrinsic ideology (luxury goods and cult objects are among the partial exceptions), all literary texts do, and the ideology behind them affects what they say and how they say it, just as the ideology of the interpreter also affects how they are interpreted. Removing ideology from evidence is sometimes just not possible, because the ideology is part of the evidence. In their discussion of ancient Assyrian inscriptions, the authors discuss very competently the imperial ideology behind the inscriptions, and when they expound the biblical narrative, they also explain what its ideology is (though they do not use the term). How they are dealing in either case with the evidence first and the ideology second is not clear to me. But perhaps Provan's critique only applies to the ideology of the interpreter, in which case every scholar will agree that such an ideology should either be suppressed or, if that is impossible, declared.

Provan regards the emphasis on social-scientific methods rather than on narrative as a symptom of a move from philosophy to science in the writing of history (18ff.). The eighteenth–nineteenth-century view that history writing can reveal truth about the past is dismissed as "positivistic" (23). In light of this claim, I understand Provan to be rejecting archaeology too. Historical-critical work on the biblical narrative is equally a symptom of this malaise, and its results a delusion. The collapse of positivistic history invites one of three responses: denial, the postmodern position that no history can in fact be written, or the third option: his own. By "positivistic" I take Provan to mean quasi-scientific knowledge. Unfortunately, he does not distinguish this from the qualified "probabilistic" knowledge that I regard as characteristic of the social sciences and of history. If he in turn is insisting that such knowledge is not certain, scientific knowledge, he is correct, and many modern historians would probably agree.

Equally incapable, in Provan's view, of providing certain knowledge is literary-historical criticism, including genre criticism. On these grounds he criticizes Soggin (1985, 26–31) for beginning his *History* with David and Solomon, and Miller and Hayes (1986, 58–79) for beginning with the monarchy. Provan points out that that Genesis–Kings forms a single continuous narrative with no literary distinction between Genesis–Joshua and what follows that would justify such a starting point. This is correct, and an important point. Creation, the flood, and the tower of Babel are, as the biblical narrative presents them, on a par with David and Solomon. However, when the authors present their own biblical history, they begin with Abraham, on the grounds that this is where the history of Israel really begins, but this seems to be equally arbitrary. The biblical history of Israel either begins (implicitly) with the institution of the Sabbath in Genesis 1, or, more strictly, Jacob, the true ancestor of Israel and father of its twelve tribal eponyms. Abraham is the ancestor of several nations besides Israel. Moreover, neither Soggin nor Miller and Hayes really depend entirely on a literary judgment: both take archaeology into account in choosing where to begin, though as we have seen, Provan rejects this procedure also.

Having made it clear where he does *not* find knowledge about Israel's history, he then offers his own source: "testimony." What he means by this—again, as it seems to me—is what I have defined in this book as cultural memory. In his own words, "storytelling is defined as "testimony": "all testimony about the past is interpretation of the past" (37). But he does not use the term or analyze cultural memory. Rather, he seems to identify it as the proper source of knowledge about the past.

Hence, "History is *fundamentally* openness to acceptance of accounts of the past that enshrine other people's memories" (47, italics in original). This is, he says, how we get knowledge of the world in general. Correct, but such knowledge includes gossip, rumor, urban myth, and much else that is not factually correct and which a historian would want to interrogate. But Provan does not accept any method for interrogation. The formulation "accounts of the past that enshrine other people's memories" is also unclear: are there "accounts of the past" that do *not* "enshrine other people's memories," such as stories of creation? If these too are "testimony," they are not based on any knowledge or experience. "Testimony" is, I suggest, an ambiguous word since it implies some kind of access on the part of the testifier to knowledge about the past. Finally, it is not clear whether Provan's comments are meant to apply to all stories about the past or just biblical ones. I assume he means all stories because he offers no argument for regarding biblical narratives as distinctive in this respect. Considering Provan's strictures about positivistic knowledge, his understanding of testimony as knowledge is extremely fuzzy and requires some more careful explanation.

But perhaps the objection is to what he sees as an a priori dismissal of stories as historical evidence. If so, then his "openness" to "statements about the past" does not mean we should necessarily believe them but simply entertain the possibility that they might be reliable. Historians should indeed be open to any potential source, but will then try to move to a judgment about their value. Whitelam's conclusions about the biblical narrative include acknowledgment, however grudging it seems, that the narrative sometimes agrees with archaeology, and his conclusion is determined by other evidence that he thinks weighs against the narrative. Nothing suggests he is initially closed to the narrative, nor are Soggin, Hayes, or Miller. But unless "openness" implies a willingness to concede that an account of the past may be wrong as well as right, it is merely prejudice. There can, after all, be false testimony too. Given his dismissal of social-scientific, literary-critical, and other "positivistic" forms of knowledge, however, it seems that only internal contradiction or implausibility is left to guide the historian from openness to belief. Unfortunately, internal contradiction is not discussed, and plausibility is rejected as a criterion (see below); the impression is thus given that "openness" has nowhere else to go but belief. This is not, then, an account of a critical history, and so, it seems to me, is not really "history" at all as we nowadays mean it (an account of what we judge "really happened"), since certain knowledge of the past is impossible (Provan 2003, 51ff.). Provan's procedure is in fact much closer to the way in which cultural memory is received.

Provan asks, "Why should verification be a principle?" "Why rush headlong into skepticism?" (55); and on his terms there cannot be any verification. But he does not make it clear why, if we should not "rush headlong into skepticism," we should rush headlong into credulity either. Are there reports that seem intrinsically unlikely? In Provan's view, we cannot say what "common human experience" is and cannot rule out something on the grounds of improbability. "No good reason, then, exists to believe that just because one testimony does not violate our sense of what is normal and possible, it is more likely to be true than another, nor to believe that an account that describes the unique or unusual is for that reason to be suspected of unreliability" (72). But surely, for the same reason, it is not to be suspected of reliability, either. Provan provides us with no basis for reading Livy's *History of Rome* as a more accurate account of the past than Apuleius's "Golden Ass," in which the narrator is metamorphosed into an animal, or to reject testimonies to sightings of Elvis Presley after his death. He says that "judgment is needed" in making such decisions (73), but he does not tell us on what any such judgment can be based and seems to have systematically excluded all the foundations on which such judgments could be made.

He nevertheless makes judgments of his own: for example, that by the end of the second millennium literacy was widespread (60). But how does he get this (positivistic) knowledge? Not, surely, from the biblical testimony—nor from Assyrian records, or from archaeology, since he has ruled out the use of such evidence, and in any case, the majority conclusion of that evidence is that literacy in Palestine was *not* widespread.

Paradoxically enough, Provan's position leads him very close to Thompson's. Though starting from diametrically opposite positions and drawing different implications on the way, both end up in the same place, severing any connection between biblical narrative and a critically determined history. The extremes of both the maximal and minimal options meet here in placing the biblical narrative beyond the competence of historical enquiry. This position fits quite well with the postmodern view that no narrative can claim to be history, but not all postmodernists deny the possibility of historical knowledge. Used critically, narratives can sometimes yield historical data. Provan says that "the biblical accounts must be appreciated first as narratives before they can be used as historical sources" (93). My impression is that all the best historical critics agree with him, and begin by reading the narrative *as narrative*; it is standard procedure to try and understand what your source is telling you before you evaluate it. Attentive reading of the narrative is what exposes the differences in ideology, language, fact, and description that enable the transition to history to be commenced. But on his own arguments Provan will not, and cannot, move beyond the narrative to do history: the narrative is the beginning and the end of the matter.

Can we discover more easily from the historical reconstruction that occupies the second part of this book how the three authors convert the biblical narrative to history? Having seen criteria of plausibility dismissed both when used by others (Soggin) and in principle (see above), we encounter a section headed "Is the Biblical Account of David's Rise Plausible?" (225). As already mentioned, the history also begins, arbitrarily, with Abraham, which is not where the biblical story starts. External data are also discussed and evaluated. We have, in fact, a fairly typical mid-twentieth-century history, and the methodological discussion, while taking account of minimalist arguments and procedures, does not result in a new or better kind of history but seems to fall back into a traditional mold, with the extra disadvantage of contradicting its stated principles in the process.

I have been obliged to spend more time on this book largely because I find it incoherent and therefore very hard to summarize and evaluate accurately, let alone fairly. It is not strictly a biblical history (for that we can read the Bible itself), but is biblical in the sense that it retells the biblical narrative (at least, from Abraham onward) along with a usually inconsequential discussion of epigraphic and archaeological evidence—inconsequential because it never seems able to make any difference to how the narrative is evaluated. Most adherents of the maximalist option would, I think, like Kofoed, espouse a more positive view of the competence of biblical criticism and, indeed, a more positive evaluation of archaeology than Provan. Unlike Provan, most maximalists still want to do biblical history as history is normally understood and, indeed, would find the notion of a Homeric history of Greece or a Virgilian history of Rome rather quaint.

Kenneth Kitchen

I have characterized Kitchen's *On the Reliability of the Old Testament* (2003) as "confrontation" because he takes head on the foundation of the minimalist option: that archaeology brings the biblical narrative into doubt as a historical record. The book has been largely ignored by serious historians and archaeologists (but see Isbell 2004), perhaps because of its gratuitous abuse of others and partly because its position is somewhat extreme. But it should be assessed because it demonstrates a great deal about the potential and the limitations of a certain use of the maximalist option.

Kitchen's treatment of the biblical text divides it into four categories: (a) where it is confirmed, (b) where it is not, (c) where it is consistent with the background, and (d) where it is misunderstood. Importantly, there are no categories of "where it is incorrect" or "where it is self-contradictory." He opens with confirmation in the sequence of Israelite and Judean monarchs in Kings and Chronicles and the references to foreign monarchs, and Israelite and Judean monarchs mentioned in foreign sources. He proceeds to outline the history of Judah from the sixth century onward and its agreement with what we know from outside the Bible. The majority of those who take the minimalist option will actually find little to object to here, except perhaps in assuming Ezra and Nehemiah to be totally reliable. Then he moves to the more problematic cases: Saul, David, and Solomon. Here he cites references to David in the Tel Dan stele, the Mesha stele, and a "Dwt" from Sheshonq. The first two of these have been discussed in chapter 5: the first reference is possible; the second contested; the third, Kitchen's own contribution, entirely speculative. At least the degrees of possibility of each might have been registered, but a lot of Kitchen's rhetoric deals in black-and-white. Perhaps probability is a principle that, like Provan, might tend to erode his case, which is, in the end, not about degrees of reliability.

Where confirmation is lacking, Kitchen usually explains why it is lacking: the Assyrians and Egyptians, for example, were not interested in Palestine in the time of David and Solomon, though the Sheshonq stele from Karnak is used as evidence in favor of the biblical account. Lacking any direct confirmation, Kitchen holds that the cultural background of the united monarchy fits the available data. But the evidence is not all considered—the survey data on population density and distribution and the excavation archaeology of early Iron I and early Iron II Jerusalem are ignored.

Where the biblical narrative is generally taken by others to be wrong, the text does not, according to Kitchen, mean what it says, or it is misunderstood. So there is no biblical account of a conquest but only of an initial assault: "The fact is that biblical scholars have allowed themselves to be swept away by the upbeat, rhetorical element present in Joshua, a persistent feature of most war reports in ancient Near Eastern sources that they are not accustomed to understand and properly handle" (163). "Understanding" presumably means knowing that a text does not always mean what it says, but most historians are in any case well aware of ancient literary conventions and Kitchen's accusation is as hyperbolic as Joshua's. He agrees, then, that Joshua is distorted, yet argues that such distortion is common to the rhetoric of ancient records of this kind. The relevance of this plea is perhaps obscure, but if we accept it, should we not expect to find distortion in the description of David's kingdom or Solomon's temple, or his wisdom, or his wives? If distortion is a common cultural element, does that not make a good case for a minimalist option? Kitchen does not follow this reasoning because, as far as I can tell, such factors are only recognized as a possibility when there is a problem in the biblical narrative. As long as we do not have any reason to doubt it, such cultural features can be disregarded.

Jericho and Ai, the highlights of the "conquest" problem, do not impose such a necessity. Jericho was a tiny town, "an appendage to its spring and oasis," of only symbolic value. Yet according to Joshua 6 it had a king and a garrison, and gold, silver, and other booty. We might respond: "some 'appendage'!" The destruction of Ai cannot be explained by Kitchen, and so is "enigmatic" (188)—yet only enigmatic on Kitchen's premise that the biblical account cannot be mistaken. Other historians might find the enigma in Kitchen's own ideology, not that of the text. Such an ideology at any rate compels him to even more curious deductions, of which I give two examples. In Exodus 6:3 Yhwh reveals himself to Moses by his name, and says that this name was not previously disclosed. "I *did not make myself known,*" he says. Kitchen suggests that this really means "I *did*" (a "rhetorical negative"). The second example concerns Isaiah 40–55, usually regarded as the work of a Second Isaiah dated to the early Persian period. Since Kitchen does not believe that anyone other than Isaiah wrote the whole book in the eighth century BCE, the Cyrus to whom these chapters refer is a different Cyrus from the sixth-century conqueror of Babylon (for these and further examples, see the review by Isbell). In short, it is hard to find any case where Kitchen is prepared to even entertain the possibility that the text might be incorrect, and for this reason he is widely considered to be a fundamentalist, dogmatically committed to biblical inerrancy. But this is not true: we have seen that he is willing to accept that the text does not mean what it says, and of Saul's age at accession (1 Sam. 13:1) he comments that the figure is "clearly defective" (309). If this means "wrong," then Kitchen is obviously not a fundamentalist, and, more importantly, he has told us that the Old Testament is not 100 percent reliable.

Kitchen deals also with the pentateuchal narratives, all datable to the second millennium, but while he dates the Sinai documents to the fourteenth or thirteenth century, he recognizes that the Hebrew in which they are written did not then exist (he fails to explain why they should be written in a Canaanite dialect anyway rather than either the Aramaic of the patriarchs or the Egyptian of their homeland for four hundred years). The answer is that they were recopied. This brings us to the question of how we got our Bible, but we do not get any further discussion, other than the implication that the recopying was exact, contrary to all the manuscript and text-critical evidence we actually have which shows recopying to have been sometimes editorially creative and always generating textual variation.

Apart from the implausible pretexts offered for many apparent inaccuracies, Kitchen makes only half his case. Showing that names of several monarchs match up and that many events are not implausible does not take us much beyond Kofoed's critique, which is both better informed and also avoids abusing opponents in the process. Mostly, Kitchen does not verify much more than the possibility of a plausible setting. Genuine confirmation is surprisingly thin, given his claims. More serious problems lie in the areas and issues he does not address, including a lot of survey archaeology and the entire range of literary-critical work on the biblical text, which Kitchen obviously rejects but does not directly engage. Furthermore, he seems to take every statement about the past as referential, assuming it is supposed to be historically accurate. He does not consider other ways in which the Bible, like other ancient texts, deals with the past. For example, he ignores (like Provan et al.) the early stories of Genesis. Does he regard the creation of the world or the universal flood as reliable accounts, or do they represent something different? Did all languages originate in Babel? Are such stories reliable? If so, how do we defend that conclusion, and if not, how, if at all, can we distinguish a non-reliable biblical story from the reliable ones? All we have from Kitchen is an assertion that these early Genesis narratives are very ancient. But their antiquity means nothing; it does not follow that they are therefore reliable, though somehow this seems to be implied. But does Kitchen claim total reliability or should we be considering what degrees of reliability—in which case there is a debate to be had over his arguments and conclusions (and the title of his book)?

To be fair, Kitchen makes a good case for being less negative about the possibly historical value of some biblical narratives than most scholars allow, and at times his detailed attention suggests that the historian can do more with certain parts of the biblical narrative than is usually done. He is right, for example, to show that the biblical account of the entry into Canaan is not strictly speaking as contradictory as is often suggested. But the details he presents are not made to add up to a coherent case for a certain degree of reliability because of the lack of any overall explanation of what the biblical narratives are, where they come from, how they work, how they have been transmitted, and what we mean by "reliability."

Kitchen, it must be said, is a good Egyptologist but not a biblical scholar, nor an Assyriologist. He is well-informed about matters beyond his own expertise, but mostly secondhand, and he is not in a position to pass his frequent verdicts of stupidity or ignorance on others who are better qualified in their own field. The result of his many dismissive comments about others may well be that his work is hardly reviewed at all by serious scholars but is welcomed only by those without the knowledge to appreciate its deficiencies.

Summary

I cannot disguise the fact that I regard the minimalist option as a very soundly based and well-argued position. Unfortunately only one of the three maximalist accounts I have reviewed seems to me to engage responsibly with the discipline of history as I have outlined it in this book. Kofoed probably puts the case as most maximalists would, and as well as it can be put. But he does not claim to render the minimalist option invalid, and I have encountered no thesis which succeeds in doing that. On the other hand, some advocates of a thoroughly minimalist option regard the maximalism as methodologically invalid. In my view (which may be in a minority west of the Atlantic), the maximalist view requires more stringent defense. I believe it is possible, and desirable, that the best arguments for such an option should be provided.

Kofoed's call for further research, then, can be endorsed. There is an increasing tendency for a minimalist option to be preferred for the Pentateuch, for Joshua and Judges, and even for 1–2 Samuel. But the books of Kings offer scope for comparison of some Judean accounts with those of other parties. These comparisons enable us to assess the quality of memories shown to be derived directly or indirectly from historical events. But we have also to explain divergences, which means considering the relationship between what we can know of the past and what the narratives as a whole say, rather than highlighting individual cases. In short, we need to establish the right way to understand what these narratives are doing with the past. The differences between the minimalist and maximalist options are not ultimately about how much is true—that is the outcome, and not the starting point of the method—but what role historical truth plays in the construction of these narratives and in their meaning.

It is important that we continue to pursue every realistic and rational way of doing biblical history with all the available sources, for what we historically "know" is far less than what we do not know, both about the history of ancient Israel and Judah and about the origins and history of the biblical stories. Extreme minimalism and maximalism have their place here, if only to remind us of the limits of reason and the extent of imagination, of the fragility of historical "knowledge" from any source. Most importantly, however, misguided and unhelpful rhetoric that fuels opposition between the options needs to be discarded in favor of collaboration on a common task that will never be finalized. For history marches on.

References

Ahlström, Gösta W.
>   1993 *The History of Ancient Palestine from the Palaeolithic Period to Alexander's Conquest*, Sheffield: Sheffield Academic Press.

Banks, Diane
>   2006 *Writing the History of Israel*, London: T&T Clark.

Barr, James
>   2000 *History and Ideology in the Old Testament*, Oxford: Oxford University Press.

Brettler, Marc
>   1995 *The Creation of History in Ancient Israel*, London: Routledge.

Bright, John
>   1959 *A History of Israel*, Philadelphia: Westminster Press (4th ed., Louisville, KY: Westminster John Knox Press, 2000).

Coote, R. B., and K. W. Whitelam
>   1987 *The Emergence of Early Israel in Historical Perspective*, Sheffield: Almond Press.

Davies, Philip R.
>   1992 *In Search of Ancient Israel*, Sheffield: Sheffield Academic Press.
>   2007 *The Origins of Biblical Israel*, London: T&T Clark.

de Geus, Cornelius H. J.
>   1976 *The Tribes of Israel: An Investigation into Some of the Presuppositions of Martin Noth's Amphictyony Hypothesis*, Assen: Van Gorcum.

Garbini, Giovanni
>   1988 *History and Ideology in the Old Testament*, London: SCM Press, New York: Crossroad.

Gottwald, Norman K.
>   1979 *The Tribes of Yahweh: A Sociology of the Religion of Liberated Israel*, Maryknoll, NY: Orbis.

Grabbe, Lester L.
>   2007 *Ancient Israel: What Do We Know and How Do We Know It?* London: T&T Clark.

Isbell, Charles David
2004 Review of Kitchen, *On the Reliability of the Old Testament*, http://www
.bibleinterp.com/articles/Isbell-Kitchen_and_Minimalism.htm.

Kitchen, Kenneth A.
2003 *On the Reliability of the Old Testament*, Grand Rapids: Eerdmans.

Kofoed, Jens Bruun
2005 *Text History: Historiography and the Study of the Biblical Text*, Winona Lake,
Ind.: Eisenbrauns.

Lemche, Niels Peter
1977 "The Greek 'Amphictyony'—Could It Be a Prototype for the Israelite
Society in the Period of the Judges?" *Journal for the Study of the Old Testament* 4:48–59.

1985 *Early Israel: Anthropological and Historical Studies on the Israelite Society before
the Monarchy*, Leiden: Brill.

1988 *Ancient Israel: A New History of Israelite Society*, Sheffield: Sheffield Academic Press.

2001 "The Old Testament—A Hellenistic Book?" in L. L. Grabbe (ed.), *Did
Moses Speak Attic? Jewish Historiography and Scripture in the Hellenistic
Period*, Sheffield: Sheffield Academic Press, 287–318.

Mendenhall, George E.
1973 *The Tenth Generation: The Origins of the Biblical Tradition*, Baltimore: Johns
Hopkins University Press.

Miller, J. Maxwell, and John H. Hayes
1986 *A History of Ancient Israel and Judah*, Philadelphia: Westminster Press,
London: SCM Press (2nd ed., Louisville, KY: Westminster John Knox
Press, 2006).

Moore, Megan Bishop
2006 *Philosophy and Practice in Writing a History of Ancient Israel*. London: T&T
Clark.

Nicholson, Ernest
2004 "Current 'Revisionism' and the Literature of the Old Testament," in John
Day (ed.), *In Search of Pre-Exile Israel: Proceedings of the Oxford Old Testament Seminar*, London: T&T Clark, 1–22.

Noth, Martin
1958 *The History of Israel*, London: A&C Black (German 1950).

Provan, I., V. Phillips Long, and Tremper Longman
2003 *A Biblical History of Israel*, Louisville, KY: Westminster John Knox Press.

Soggin, J. Alberto
1985 *A History of Israel: From the Beginnings to the Bar Kochba Revolt, AD 135*,
London: SCM Press.

Thompson, Thomas L.
   1974   *The Historicity of the Patriarchal Narratives*, Berlin: de Gruyter.
   1992   *Early History of the Israelite People: From the Written and Archaeological Sources*, Leiden: Brill.
   1999   *The Bible in History: How Writers Create a Past*, London: Jonathan Cape (U.S. edition: *The Mythic Past: Biblical Archaeology and the Myth of History*, New York: Basic Books).

Van Seters, John
   1975   *Abraham in History and Tradition*, New Haven, Conn.: Yale University Press.

Whitelam, Keith W.
   1996   *The Invention of Ancient Israel: The Silencing of Palestinian History*, London: Routledge.

Wright, G. E.
   1952   *God Who Acts: Biblical Theology as Recital*, London: SCM Press.

Young, Ian, Robert Rezetko, and Martin Ehrensvard
   2008   *Linguistic Dating of Biblical Texts*, London: Equinox.

Part Three

Reflections

Chapter Nine

History, Memory, and Theology

I have said little about the role of theology in biblical history since the opening chapter, and I believe it has no role in the writing of a modern critical history. But it does have a role in understanding the past. It is also a factor in many people's attitudes toward the historicity of the Bible.

I started this book noting that biblical history is hardly ever taught in university faculties of history, but in departments of theology or religion. It is thus usually integrated into a biblical studies curriculum as part of an education about the Bible itself and therefore taught as part of either Judaism or Christianity. This is a pity, because if, as is often said, the Bible is one parent of Western civilization, then knowledge and understanding of what it contains should not be confined to religious believers. General ignorance of the Bible is enough of a problem even among believers in the twenty-first century anyway.

How can the Bible be read by Christian, Jew, Muslim, other religious believer, or nonbeliever? Those of the Abrahamic faiths will read it for its religious values; others may not do so as readily, and indeed even many believers will resist some of its values, including its attitudes toward women, slavery, and violence. What about reading it as history?

Those who take the Bible very seriously as history need to know that its authors did not set a good example. I have shown earlier in this book how even parts of the Bible seem to be creating or creatively rewriting history. Two thousand years ago there was already disagreement about how the biblical stories of the past should be understood. In the first century CE the historian Josephus could speak of Jewish history as being reliable because it was authored by prophets, but in Alexandria his elder contemporary Philo was treating the pentateuchal stories as allegories. The rabbis elevated Torah above prophecy and regarded the Latter Prophets (Isaiah–Malachi) as teachers of Torah. The Former Prophets had a much less obvious role; in the midrashim they are generally cited as illustrative of halakah (how to live as a Jew)—hence, homiletical. Theologically, the historical books of the Bible are the least important in Judaism. But the Torah, of course, also contains history, and the call of Abraham, the exodus, and lawgiving are central to Jewish life and identity. However, even these are subject to the same treatment: these nonlegal portions provide illustrations of how to live as a good Jew, or how not to live as a bad Jew.

For Christians, once the decision was made to retain the Jewish Scriptures in the canon, the historical books posed a problem. The law had been partly superseded, but much of it remained in force, while the Prophets (and some psalms) foretold Christ; the wisdom texts were also still valid as ethical instruction, and the psalms were appropriate for Christian devotion, too. All of this literature made sense as Christian Scripture. What was to be done, theologically, with the historical books? As in early Judaism, the options were either to treat them as a preparation for the gospel, a record of the divine plan to prepare the world for the coming of its Savior, or to treat them allegorically, to see them as prototypes (Jonah of the resurrection, Hannah as the proto-Mary, Samson's breaking out of Gaza as Jesus breaking the bars of hell).

Until the end of the Middle Ages, biblical texts were assigned plural meanings within Christianity, including the literal, allegorical, tropological (as pertaining to present everyday life), and analogical (as indicating the end of history). In short, reading historical books as history remained only one option of several. And before the advent of the modern conception of history as the real past of a real world that could and should be critically discovered, the literal meaning was not at all paramount, and certainly not the issue of historicity.

The relevance of religious belief for dealing historically with the Bible is a modern one; as a nonreligious believer it does not occupy me, and I am not going to recommend to readers how to solve it. But there is a sense in which religious belief is highly relevant to the modern biblical historian's task, and I will illustrate this emically and etically. "Emic" means a view from inside: originating in social anthropology it designates a description of a society as an insider would see it. "Etic" couches the description in terms of an outside observer. There is no necessary conflict between the two, and they can usefully be seen as complementary. They provide different kinds of understanding.

A description along emic lines might be as follows: the view of the Bible itself, and of most Jews, Christians, and Muslims, is that there is a god who is unique and who has determined what happens in the world. For most Muslims and some Christians this determination comes down even to personal circumstances, even predetermination. On this view, everything that happens has a meaning and conforms to a plan. History should therefore seek to disclose the meaning of the past. One may do this in two ways: mantically or empirically. Both these techniques have their counterparts in the Bible itself. The mantic technique uses revelation; the empirical uses only observation of the natural order. The former is represented typically by prophecy, the latter by wisdom. The empirical option provides a hermeneutical basis for a religious believer to do history: by studying what has happened one can study the mind and purposes of God. The mantic option does not believe that observation alone can bring understanding; history may therefore be interesting but ultimately tells us little that is useful.

The etic view is that of a secularist (or a believer wearing a secular hat). It is that history has no intrinsic meaning, either because there is no god or there is no god of the kind that interferes in what happens on earth. But it may display patterns that illustrate human behavior. But one of the features of human historical behavior is that it is influenced by what people believe about the past. The movement of history is determined by individual and collective actions and interactions, which, where they are not necessitated by external compulsion, are the product of what people believe. To begin to understand history, then, you need to know what people believe. But what happened and what people remember as having happened are not identical. What the insider regards as the real past the outsider sees as just the insider's past. But we all need a past and all outsiders are insiders somewhere else, with their own memories of the past. We all live in our own pasts, which we share with various others. Westerners share the Bible as part of our past—*as long as we remember what its story is.*

But we also share another past—one born of inquiry and rationality, of a human-centered understanding of things—more or less, a "scientific" heritage that is definitely not biblical. So we can both feel our insider pasts and explore our external pasts. We do the latter by means of the discipline of history. The Bible is a place of conflict between these two kinds of history. In Palestine itself a vicious struggle is being fought by people who will not tolerate the difference between a real history and a cultural memory. In the West, too, there are those who insist on their own Christian cultural memory as being the real past.

The role of the historian is, I would argue, not just to find out what happened, but also to expose memories for what they are—not to dismiss them, but to enable them to perform their proper task and, more importantly, to make a contribution to a future in which histories are no longer the instruments of division and strife, but of understanding and cooperation. The bitterness of a lot of contemporary debate about biblical historicity is a symptom of the power that resides in cultural memory and its control over identity. It is a sad irony when historians, of all people, are unable to see that this clash of memories is what history can mitigate, if we pursue it with intelligence and honesty.

Index of Ancient Sources

OLD TESTAMENT

Genesis

4:17–24	27
5	27
5:28	27
6–9	31
7:4	32
7:6	31
7:24	31
8:3–4	31
8:10, 12	32
8:13–19	27
9:28–29	27
10	43
11:1–26	27
11:32	27
12	35–36, 38–39
15:13,16	28
20	38–39
26	38–39

Exodus

6:3	166
6:14–25	28
12:40	28
20:18–23:33	36

Leviticus

25	25
26:35	25

Joshua

1–11	139
6	139
6–11	139
10	139
12	139
13	139
14	139
15:20–18:1	139
15:63	41
18–19	139
18:13	127
18:22	127
18:28	41
20–22	139
23	139
24	139

Judges

1:8	41
1:21	41

1 Samuel

9:1–10:16	39

10:16–11:14	39
13:1	21, 167
14	40
16:14–23	40
17	40
17:12–31	40
17:54	41

2 Samuel

5:6	41
9–20	37

1 Kings

1–2	37, 49
8	50
11:31–32	52
12	127
15:16–22	96
22:29–38	96

2 Kings

6:12–22:40	91
8:28–29	96
9:14–16	96
12:5–16	99
13:10	23
14:1–2	23
14:23	23

2 Kings (*continued*)
15   27
16:15–29   23
17   33, 51
17:18   52
18   23
18:13–16   92
18:17–19:37   92
19   44
20:20   97
20:22   91
22:20   91
23:22   33
25:21, 26   51

1 Chronicles
8:28   53
8:33–40   53
9:39–44   53

2 Chronicles
16:1–6   96
24:4–14   99
30:1–12   33
32:3–4   97
36:21   25, 53

Ezra
1–3   25
1–6   118, 121
1:1, 5   54
4–6   121
4:24   116
6:15   116

Nehemiah
1:1–3   118
1:3   79, 116

8–9 (10)   117
12   121
12:26   117
12:36   117
13:3   54

Psalms
78   132
106   132
136   132

Isaiah
22:9–11   97
40–55   166

Jeremiah
25:11–12   25
29:10   25

Daniel
1:19–21   40
2:24–26   40
4   120
7:25   29–30
9   28–29
9:2   25
10–12   29

Amos
4:6   44

Zechariah
1:12   25
7:5   25

NEW TESTAMENT

Matthew
1   27
1:17   26

Acts
13   22

**APOCRYPHA AND
PSEUDEPIGRAPHA**

Judith
1:1   44
4:3   44

Ben Sira
49:13   116
50:26   119

2 Maccabees
1:18–36   116, 119
2:13   116, 120

1 Esdras
3–4   121

1 Enoch
93:1–10;
  91:11–17   28–29

Biblical Antiquities   36

Jubilees   29

**DEAD SEA
SCROLLS**

11QMelchizedek   29
1QGenesis
  Apocryphon   35–36
Damascus Document 118

Index of Names

Abegg, Martin, 22
Abu el-Haj, Nadia, 62
Ahlström, Gösta, 152
Albright, W. F., 24, 62–64, 150
Alt, Albrecht, 64–65, 150–51
Appleby, Joyce, 14
Assmann, Jan, 106, 113
Auld, A Graeme, 27, 37
Avigad, Nahman, 98

Banks, Diane, 15, 150
Barnes, William H., 23
Barr, James, 159
Barton, John, 132
Bergren, Theodore A., 119
Brettler, Marc Zvi, 111, 131–33, 154
Bright, John, 150–51
Bruins, Hendrik J., 75

Coote, Robert B., 154

Davies, Philip R., 47, 98, 115, 119,
    130, 153, 156
Davis, Thomas, 60
de Geus, Cornelius H. J., 152
Dearman, J. Andrew, 94
Dever, William G., 65, 128–29, 141

Drinkard, Joel, 94
Durkheim Emile, 106

Edelman, Diana, 80, 130
Ehrensvard, Martin, 157
Elton, Geoffrey R., 14

Finkelstein, Israel, 66–67, 74–75,
    129–30
Flint, Peter, 22
Frei, Hans W., 15
Fulbrook, Mary, 14

Gaili, Gershon, 23–24
Garbini, Giovanni, 152
Gottwald, Norman K., 66, 151
Grabbe, Lester L., 117, 124–26,
    142, 150

Halbwachs, Maurice, 106
Halpern, Baruch, 89, 125, 132
Hammer, Olav, 111
Hayes, John H., 24, 150, 152, 160,
    162
Herzog, Ze'ev, 58–9, 75
Higham, Thomas, 71
Hooker, Paul K., 24

181

Hughes, Jeremy, 28, 31
Hunt, Lynn, 14

Isbell, Charles David, 164, 167

Jacob, Margaret, 14
Jones, Sian, 81

Keller, Werner H., 16
Kitchen, Kenneth, 164–71
Knauf, E. Axel, 89, 139–40
Kofoed, Jens Bruun, 157–58, 164, 167, 169

Larsson, Gerhard, 32
Lemaire, André, 95
Lemche, Niels Peter, 151–52, 156
Levy, Thomas E., 71
Lewis, James R., 111
Lipschits, Oded, 79, 93
Liverani, Mario, 114
Long, Burke O., 62
Long, V. Phillips, 158–64
Longman, Tremper, 158–64

Marx, Karl, 16
Mazar, Amihai, 75–6
Mazar, Eilat, 75–6
McKenzie, Steven L., 37
Mendels, Doron, 115
Mendenhall, George E., 66, 151
Millard, Alan, 85
Miller, J. Maxwell, 150, 152, 160, 162
Miller, James C., 81
Moore, Megan Bishop, 6, 155

Na'aman, Nadav, 91–2
Nicholson, Ernest W., 157
Noth, Martin, 47, 63–65, 150–52

Provan, Iain, 158–65

Rezetko, Robert, 157
Robinson, Edward, 60
Rogerson, J. W., 98
Routledge, Bruce, 94

Sass, Benjamin, 99
Sayce, A. H., 60–61
Shavit, Ya'acov, 62
Shenkel, J. D., 26
Silberman, Neil Asher, 60, 67, 129–30
Singer-Avitz, Lily, 75
Smith, Mark S., 111
Soggin, J. A., 152, 160, 162–63
Stenring, K., 32

Thiele, Edwin B., 23
Thompson, Thomas L., 30, 65, 95, 151–53, 156

Ulrich, Eugene, 22
Ussishkin, David, 75

van der Plicht, Johannes, 75
Van Seters, John, 37, 65, 151
von Rad, Gerhard, 129, 151
von Ranke, Leopold, 16

Weber, Max, 16
Wellhausen, Julius, 24–25, 61
White, Hayden, 15
Whitelam, Keith W., 5, 154, 156, 158–59
Wright, G. Ernest, 64, 151

Yadin, Yigael, 66
Young, Ian, 157